"Empowering Educators: The Impact of an ICT Skills Development Program on Computer Self-Efficacy and Course Outcomes

C.miya

Hi, Dad!
waves To my greatest father in the world and my mother.and my
colleagues who assist me in creating this endeavor

Contents

1. Preface

   Chapter1 **INTRODUCTION**

   Chapter2 REVIEW OF RELATED LITERATURE

2. Chapter3 EMERGENCE OF THE PROBLEM

   Chapter4 DEVELOPMENT AND DESCRIPTION OF THE TOOLS

3. Chapter5 METHOD OF THE STUDY

4. Copyright
5. Acknowledgement

Preface

hello "wave" I am the book's editor. This book came from our publishing company.Every book I must read for my job, and I'd like you to inform me that this one is worthwhile without further ado, there is an introduction.

This Digital century is associated with the explosion of knowledge based countries, villages, towns and cities where ICT may play an eminent role. Specially, in educational community, information and communication technology skills have become crucial to the curriculum designing and implementation. With the internet, computer and mobile technology available to most of the teachers, education technology becomes increasingly indispensable in the field of education. Availability of the internet in schools enables teachers and students to have a variety of opportunities to expand the curriculum. In the digital age public schools will require teachers to have competent technology skills and be able to effectively implement technology in classrooms.

The introduction and rapid spread of information and communication technology, such as email, telephone, fibre optics and EDUSAT, is revolutionising the way in which societies interact, conduct their classes, committed to their human resource development agendas. ICT society enables enormous opportunities for enhancing business and economic viability at reduced cost. It also contributes in strengthening democracy, increasing social participation, competing in global education and removing barrier to modernisation. ICT is a powerful tool to bring up reform in education, as it allows students to participate in a wide range of computer activities, while home serves as a complementary site for regular engagement in narrower set of computer activities. ICT is being applied successfully in instructional methods, learning, teaching and evaluation, and has been shown to raise educational standards and connect learning to real life situations.

Teleconferencing classrooms allow both learner and teacher to interact simultaneously with ease and convenience, and multipurpose resources are abundant on the internet. ICT assists in transforming a teaching environment into a learner centred one, and learners are authorized by teachers to make decisions, plans and so forth. The National Curriculum Framework (NCF) 2005 has also been developed to incorporate ICT into the curriculu

LIST OF TABLES

Table No.	Title	Page No.
4.1	Distribution of items of computer self-efficacy scale in various domains	88
4.2	Distribution of dimension wise items of the first draft	93
4.3	t- ratio for technology integration beliefs scales of the first draft	94
4.4	Blue print of specification of achievement test (First draft)	98
4.5	Difficulty value and discriminating powers of the items in the draft of computer achievement test	100-101
4.6	Distribution of discriminating powers of the items of first draft of computer achievement test after first try out	101
4.7	Distribution of discriminating power of items of the first draft of computer achievement test after second try-out	102
4.8	Blue print of final draft of computer achievement test	102-103
5.1	Diagrammatic Presentation Of The Study	105
5.2	College Wise Distribution Of Sample	107
5.3	Distribution Of Students According To The Treatment	107
5.4	Name of student for experimental and control group for experimental treatment	109-111
5.5	Details of conduct of Instructional Program	113
6.1	t. ratio for mean pre test computer self efficacy score control group	120
6.2	A summary of Descriptive statistics for computer self efficacy scores of and Control group	122

6.2 (a)	A summary of Descriptive statistics for computer self efficacy scores of experimental group	123
6.3	t. ratio for mean pre test computer self efficacy score experimental group	125
6.4	Showing pre-test mean and standard deviation of experimental and control group on self regulation	130
6.5	A summary of Descriptive statistics of experimental group on pre-test and post-test scores on self regulation	132

6.6	Significance of difference between mean gain scores of experimental and control group on self regulation	136
6.7	t-value for the difference in the pre test mean scores of experimental and control groups on technology integration beliefs	142
6.8	A summary of Descriptive statistics for technology integration beliefs control group and experimental group	144
6.9	t - ratio for difference in mean gain scores of experimental and control group on technology integration beliefs	145
6.10	Significance of difference between mean pre test score of experimental and control group on computer achievement	147
6.11	A summary of Descriptive statistics for Computer Achievement	149
6.12	t - ratio for difference in mean gain scores of experimental and control group on Computer Achievement	150
6.13	Showing significance difference between the post test mean score of experimental and control group on course satisfaction	153

LIST OF FIGURES

Figure No	Title	Page No.
1.1	Relationship between ICT development at a school and approaches to ICT-related teaching and learning. Based on Anderson and Weert (2002)	9
1.2	ICT framework	14
1.3	Outcome pyramid for quality centre national accreditation committee	27
1.4	Inverted assessment pyramid	29
5.1	Diagrammatic Presentation Of The Study	107
6.1	A bar diagram depicting pre-test scores on computer self efficacy for Experimental and control group	121
6.2	A Bar diagram depicting difference in pre-test and post-test scores on computer self efficacy for Experimental group	123
6.3	A bar diagram depicting difference in pre-test and post-test scores on computer self efficacy for control group	124
6.4	Bar diagram showing comparison of gain score of experimental and control group on various dimensions of computer self efficacy	126
6.5	Bar diagram showing comparison of post test scores of experimental and control group on various dimensions of self regulation	131

6.6	Bar diagram showing comparison of mean Pre-test and post-test scores of control group on various dimensions of self regulation	133
6.7	Bar diagram showing comparison of mean Pre-test and post-test scores of experimental group on various dimensions of self regulation	134
6.8	Bar diagram showing comparison of mean gain scores of experimental and control group on various dimensions of self regulation	137
6.9	Bar diagram showing comparison of mean scores of experimental and control group on technology integration beliefs	143
6.10	Bar diagram showing comparison of mean scores of experimental and control group on technology integration beliefs	144
6.11	Bar diagram showing comparison of Means Gain Scores of Experimental and Control Groups on technology integration beliefs	146
6.12	Bar diagram showing comparison of Means Pre-test Scores of Experimental and Control Groups on computer achievement test	148

6.13	Bar diagram showing comparison of Means Pre-test and post-test Scores of Experimental and Control Groups on computer achievement test	149
6.14	Bar diagram showing comparison of Mean Gain Scores of Experimental and Control Groups on Computer Achievement	151
6.15	Bar diagram showing comparison of mean scores of experimental and control group on course satisfaction	153

LIST OF ABBREVIATIONS

ANOVA	Analysis of Variance
CSE	Computer Self efficacy
CSQ	Course Satisfaction Questionnaire
Ctrl	Control
df	Degree of freedom
DP	Discriminating Power
DV	Difficulty Value
Exp	Experimental
H	Hypothesis
ICT	Information and Communication Technology
IT	Information Technology
Kurt	Kurtosis
M	Mean
N	Number
NCF	National Curriculum Framework
SD	Standard Deviation
Skew	Skewness
SPSS	Statistical Package for Social Science
SRL	Self Regulated Learning
SRQ	Self regulation questionnaire
TIB	Technology integration beliefs
UNDP	United Nation Development Program

CHAPTER I INTRODUCTION

1.1.1   This Digital century is associated with the explosion of knowledge based country, villages, town and cities wherein ICT may play an eminent role. Specially, in educational community, information and communication technology skills have become crucial to the curriculum designing and implementation. With the internet, computer and mobile technology available to most of the teachers, education technology becomes increasingly indispensable in the field of education. In today's smarts school there are multimedia software, content based CD ROMS, online resources tools, vast wealth of information, shared professional practices (Keane, 2002) communication tools and new strategies of learning. Availability of the internet in schools enables teachers and students to have a variety of opportunities to expand the curriculum. In modern era, school are challenged by increased visibility, accessibility, roles and cost of educational technology. Considering current scenario in education, a modern classroom would not be complete without computers software, internet connections, projector and a variety of other high tech devices (Keane, 2002). According to Hasselbring (2000) in near future, schools will be well equipped with the best hardware and software technologies. But it is matter of concern that teachers and students will use them effectively, if teachers are not well trained. The success of technology integration in schools depends on training both in service and pre service teachers. In the digital age public schools will require teachers to have competent technology skills and be able to effectively implement technology in classrooms. Therefore it is logical to require pre service teachers to incorporate technology into the teaching classroom. The introduction and rapid spread of information and communication technology, such as email, telephone, fibre optics and EDUSAT is revolutionising the way in which societies interact, conduct their classes, committed to their human resource development agendas. ICT society enables enormous opportunities for enhancing business and economic viability at reduced cost. ICT also contributes in strengthening democracy, increasing social participation, competing in global education and removing barrier to modernisation. The most common Information and communication technology tools which are used in today's education are computers, internet, email, radio, television and projectors. Kent and Facer (2004) described school as an important place in which students participate in wide range of computer activities, while home serves as a complementary site for regular engagement in narrower set of computer activities. These days ICT is being applied successfully in instructional methods, learning, teaching and evaluation. ICT is considered as a powerful tool to bring up reform at a larger extent. A large number of previous studies have shown that an appropriate use of ICT can raise educational standard and connect learning to the real life situations. ICT tends to expand access to education (Lowther, 2008 & Tantall, 2005). Through ICT, learning can occur 24 hours a day, seven days a week and anywhere in the world. Teleconferencing classrooms allow both learner and teacher to interact simultaneously with ease and convenience. Multipurpose resource are abundant on the internet, and knowledge can be acquired through video clips on You tube, audio sound, visual presentation and so on. ICT assists in transforming a teaching environment into a learner centred one (Sanchez & Aleman, 2011). Since learners are actively involved in the learning process in ICT classrooms, they are authorized by teachers to make decisions, plans and so forth (Huang, Hou and Lu, 2010). The National Curriculum Framework (NCF) 2005 has highlighted the importance of ICT in an era of explosion of information and communication technologies. The twenty first century human civilization has gone towards knowledge based society. ICT can be summarized as the process, method and means of receiving and retrieving, storing and collecting, manufacturing, communicating and disseminating knowledge and information. The integration of technology into curriculum will not only include hardware devices connected to computers and software application, but also interactive digital content, internet and satellite communication devices, web based content, interactive forum, learning management system and information management systems. According to National Policy on Information and Communication Technology (ICT) in School Education (2012) throughout the world, ICT is proven as a tool for educational transformation. It can be brought into the schools in three different ways: (i) as a tool for delivering information and or services, including school administration; (ii) as a tool to teach other subjects; and (iii) as a academic curriculum subject to equip the students with skills required to succeed in the knowledge economy. From the curricular perspective we are concerned with the second and the third aspect of ICT at the school level. Some private institutions are providing ICT education as computer education. In the case of public schools, colleges and universities even the availability of computer education is very limited. Under the national curriculum, computer education is offered as an optional subject at the secondary level. However, because of resource constraints only a few public schools have been able to offer this course. The demand from the public for ICT education in school is high despite their recognition that present school curriculum is overloaded with subjects and contents. The Tenth Plan has clearly emphasized the need to develop industries and services based on information and communication technology. For this, the Plan has policy and strategy for introducing computer education from school level curriculum and providing Internet facilities in public schools and universities. Recently, HMG (1997) Secondary education perspective plan has also given a high priority to provide computer education with the slogan "Computer Education for all by 2015". This warrants for a comprehensive attempt to introduce ICT education in schools. Learning across the world is rapidly changing and bringing about this change is the use of information and communication technology (ICT) or simply computers, which has advanced the access to information and is providing richer and relevant opportunities for those who have embraced it. The use of ICT for education is revolutionising the traditional classroom and encourages the learner to progress outside of the four walls of classroom, is more personalized and has become a powerful motivational tool. However, because of the fast pace in technology development, in the span of less than a decade, students have shifted from notebooks and textbooks to laptops, iPods and net books. The National Policy on Education (1986) has laid special emphasis on the use of computers and educational technology for improving quality of education at school, college and university level. First time in the history of Indian education, Educational technology has been employed as important tool in the spread of education. It has been stated that ICT is a principal driver of economic development and social change worldwide (Kozma, 2005; Leech, 2008). According to David (1991) technology has the potential to transform the relationships between teachers and students. The educational technology has plenty of evidences to support such transformation. In the present scenario, only 2% of our manpower in the age group of 15-29 is formally skilled. However, statistics show that 90% of the employment opportunities require vocational skills which are not being imparted in the Indian school and colleges. India transitions to a knowledge based economy requires a new generation of multi skilled youth. A knowledge economy requires India to develop educationists who are flexible and analytical and who can be driving force to innovation and growth. To achieve this Indian education system should be flexible to new global environment by promoting creativity and improving the quality of education and training at all levels with the adoption of latest technology.

1.1 INFORMATION AND COMMUNICATION TECHNOLOGY

Today's world is a world of information explosion. It is matter of great concern how to cope up with such an information explosion. The very genuine answer is information technology (IT) that can help in coping with the information explosion. So it is said by researchers that information technology is nothing but coping up with explosion of information. To understand the meaning of Information and Communication Technology it should be studied separately. Information and communication technology comprises of two words. 1.1.1 Information Technology

1.1.2 Communication Technology

1.1.1 INFORMATION TECHNOLOGY

The term in its modern sense first appeared in a 1958 article published in the Harvard business review. Leavit and Whisler (2005) stated that the new technology has no single established name. Information technology is the acquisition of knowledge, processing, storage and dissemination of vocal, pictorial, textual and numerical information with the help of telecommunication. Information technology is interconnected system of equipment that is used in manipulation, transmission, computation and reception of data or information. According to Darnton and Giacoletto (1992) "Information technology is a systemic study of artefacts that can be used to give form to facts in order to provide meaning for decision making, and artefact that can be used for organization, processing, communication and application of information."

According to UNSECO (2002) "Information Technology is a scientific, technological and engineering discipline and management technique used in handing the information, it's application and association with social, economical and cultural matters."

1.1.2 COMMUNICATION TECHNOLOGY

1.1.3 Communication is an integral part of human existence. It is communication that decides the very identity of human beings. Modern society is turning into an information society and communication is the exchange of information. It is the process of transferring information from a sender to receiver via a medium in which the information is understood by both the sender and receiver. Communication Technology implies the knowledge, skills and understanding needed to exchange information verbally or non verbally. It is processing of information in terms of accessing information, decoding information and sending it via a medium and channel to the receivers. Medium or channel can be written or oral or gesture form of information through speech, action or any electronic machine. In general communication is means of connecting peoples and places.

1.1.4 INFORMATION AND COMMUNICATION TECHNOLOGY

The phrase information and communication technology has been used by academic researchers since 1980, and the abbreviation ICT became popular after it was used in a report to the UK government by Denis Stevenson in 1997. According to Wikipedia "Information and communication technology is an extended term for information technology (IT) which stresses the role of unified communication and the integration of telecommunication i.e. telephone, wireless signal, computers as well as necessary enterprise software, middleware, storage and audio visual system, which enable users to access, store, transmit and manipulate information." The term ICT is also used to refer to the convergence of audio visual and telephone networks with computer networks through a single cabling or link system. Maheswari (2002) defined ICT as "the science and activity of storing and sending information by using computers." Oxford dictionary defined ICT as "the study of the use of computer, the internet, video and other technology as subject at school."

According to Kelly (2004) "ICT refers to learning about new technologies and how to make the most effective use of the information for personal and administrative purposes." Lowe and McAuley (2002) defined "information and communication technology literacy as the skills and abilities that will enable the use of computers and related information technologies to meet personal, educational and labour market goals". Ebijuwa (2005) defined "ICT as tools used for collection, processing, storage, transmission, and dissemination of information. With advances in ICT, electronic information resources such as electronic books, electronic journals, CD-ROM databases, OPAC, Online databases and the Internet have launched the world into an information age. No institution or organization can still rely on only traditional printed information resource to perform effectively and efficiently." Roblyer and Edwards (2000) believe that the use of ICT in education has evolved from two main approaches, namely directed and constructivist instructional methods. The theoretical foundations of directed instruction are based on behaviorist learning theories and information processing theory, which is a branch of cognitive psychology. The theoretical foundations of the constructivist approaches are based on the principles of learning derived from cognitive learning theory. According to Rouse (2005) ICT is an umbrella term that includes any communication device or application, encompassing: radio, television, cellular phones, computer and network hardware and software, satellite systems and so on, as well as the various services and applications associated with them, such as videoconferencing and distance learning. ICTs are often spoken of in a particular context, such as ICTs in education, health care, or libraries. Kozma (2005) suggested three significant concerns of consideration regarding ICTs impact on education. Firstly, student outcomes such as higher scores in school subjects or the learning of entirely new skills needed for a developing economy. Secondly, teacher and classroom outcomes such as development of teachers' technology skills and knowledge of new pedagogic approaches as well as improved attitudes toward teaching should be considered. Finally, one has to consider other outcomes such as increased innovativeness in schools and access of community members to adult education and literacy. According to UNESCO (2010), the term "ICT is plural, referring to a great many technologies and it is an all encompassing term that includes the full gamut of electronic tools by means of which we gather, record and store information, and by means of which we exchange and distribute information to others." ICT is excellent tools for information processing; the new generation needs to become competent in their use, should acquire the necessary skills, and therefore must have access to computers and networks while at school (Kok, 2007). However ICT has no universal definition, as the concepts, methods and application involved in

ICT are constantly evolving on an almost daily basis.

1.1.5 CHARACTERISTICS OF ICT IN EDUCATION

According to Banerjee et al. (2012) "Globalization and technological changes have created a new global economy powered by technology, fuelled by information and driven by knowledge." The emergence of new global economy has serious implications for the nature and purpose of educational institutions. As access to information continues to grow rapidly, schools cannot be contented with the limited knowledge to be transmitted in a fixed period of time. They have to become compatible to the ever expanding knowledge and also be equipped with the technology to deal with this knowledge. According to Saomya Saxena (2013) the top ten ICT characteristics of twenty first century classroom are :

1. Active learning: In modern classroom, students are actively engaged in what they learn. Students participate in more active learning by working in groups or on computers and complete projects and other interesting activities that help them in discovering new skills.

2. Student centric: In modern classroom, the teacher serves as guide and facilitator which facilitate the learning of the students. Student's centric approach puts student's interest fist and focussed on each students need, abilities and learning styles.

3. Adaptive learning: The modern approach of adaptive learning gives students the freedom to learn at their own pace and in the way they are most comfortable with. There are number of software available in the

market for adaptive learning that teachers can use to enhance learning of the students. 4. Invitational learning: Bring your own device approach can be adopted, so that students can bring their laptops or tablets to the classroom for better personalized learning. Teaching with technological material is more effective, stimulates students' engagement, eases the work of teachers and makes it easy for students to focus on learning. 5. Student understands and follows the rules and procedure: Class rules, procedures and notices of upcoming activities should be posted in convenient places to help student to keep on the right track. The learning environment should be carefully planned and well organised. 6. Computing device: Computing devices greatly assist in teaching and learning and make it more engaging, interesting and effective. Computers not only replace the utilities of pen and paper but also give students the means to master the technology skills. 7. Collaborative learning: Teaching in isolation is very restrictive and hinders progress. Learning through collaboration is one of the most effective forms of learning. Collaborative learning includes group projects, joint problem solving, writing, debates and more. 8. Mutual respect: Teachers and students should have respect for each other. Students should not forget the value of teacher who gave them guidance. On the others hand teacher should encourage students to speak with confidence and value their opinions. 9. Performance based assessment: Regular performance based assessment should be carried out through various methods which are not restricted to written tests. Assessment should be tailored according to the abilities and needs of the students. 10. Students self learning and responsibility: Self directed students not only encourage each other, but also work with their teachers to achieve academic and behavioural goals. Teacher should employ a variety of strategies to promote responsible decision making and create self reliant students. Laudon and Laudon(2010) states that the most important drive behind Globalization is the explosion in Information and Communication Technology (ICT) sectors.

Stages of ICT Development at School Level

Anderson and Weert (2002) explained the stages of ICT

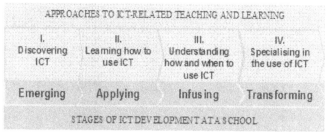

development at school level. He describes the four approaches to ICT-related teaching and learning:

Figure 1.1: Relationship between ICT development at a school and approaches to ICT related teaching and learning. Based on Anderson and Weert (2002) (1) Discovering ICT tools: ICT skills should be taught as a separate subject in the school. (2) Learning how to use ICT tools: more emphasis should be given to the development of ICT skills. It should be integrated into separate subjects. (3) Understanding the use ICT tools to achieve particular purposes: ICT should be embedded across curriculum. It should be used where demanded not everywhere. (4) Specializing in the use of ICT tools: ICT should be learned as specialized subjects or professional courses.These approaches are parallel to another axis, which describes the four stages of ICT development in a school: (1) emerging; (2) applying; (3) infusing and (4) transforming. Each stage is characterized by eight indicators: (1) vision; (2) learning pedagogy; (3) development plans and policies; (4) facilities and resources; (5) understanding of curriculum; (6) professional development for school staff; (7) community and (8) assessment. Therefore, the general model of ICT development at a school can be adapted and applied for the analysis of the notion of ICT literacy from the implemented perspective.

1.1.5 BENEFITS OF USING ICT IN EDUCATION

In teaching learning process the interaction takes place between teachers and students so management personnel requires lot of data to be stored for retrieval when required.

ICT encompasses all those gadgets that deal with the processing of information for better and effective communication. Brush, Glazewski and Hew (2008) stated that ICT is tool for students to discover learning topics, solve problems and provide solution to the problem in the efficient manner. ICT makes knowledge acquisition more accessible and understandable. Support self-directed learning: these days Students actively engaged in the use of computers and internet for making assignments (Sanchez and Aleman, 2011). They build new knowledge through accessing, selecting and interpreting information and data. It is generally believed that ICT has empowered teachers and learners to promote change and foster development in modern educational era. According to Rajan (2011) Benefits that ICT brought to education according to present research finding are: Benefits for the Teachers • ICT has facilitated sharing of resources, expertise and advice. • It has included greater flexibility in the carried out task. • It has increased teacher's gain in ICT literacy skills, confidence and enthusiasm. • ICT has made planning, preparation of lesson and designing easier for the teachers. • ICT has enhanced the professional image of the teachers. • It has also enabled teachers to help students in learning outside school hours. • ICT has enabled the teachers to get up-to date student and school information anytime and anywhere. • It has enhanced focussed teaching. Benefits for the Students According to Reid (2002) "ICT offers students more time to explore beyond the mechanics of course content allowing them to better understand concepts." • Students can get higher quality lesson through greater collaboration between teacher and students. • It has enhanced focussed learning among students.

- ICT helps the student in behavioural management.
- It has enhanced understanding and analytical skills.
- It has improved reading and writing habits of students.
- ICT has helped student in development of higher order learning styles.
- Flexibility of anytime and anywhere access (Jacobsen & Kremer, 2000).
- ICT emphasised student centric classroom.

Benefits for Parents

- ICT has made possible easier communication with parents.
- It has helped parents in getting higher quality students report: more legible, more detailed and well presented.
- ICT has helped in increasing the parent involvement in education system.
- It has helped in getting knowledge of children's learning and capabilities.
- ICT has made possible parent's engagement in school community.
- ICT has made positive impact across a very wide range of aspects.

1.1.5 The National Skill Development Policy, 2009 (NSD)

The National Skill Development Policy has an ambitious plan to skill about 12-15 million youth each year. As part of this policy and to ensure execution, the Government of India has setup the National Skill Development Mission under the chairmanship of the Honourable Prime minister of India. The Policy amongst other things proposed to establish a National Vocational Education Qualification Framework. The framework proposes the following features:-

- Competency based qualifications and certification on the basis of nationally agreed standards and criteria.
- Certification for learning achievement and qualification.
- The avoidance of duplication and overlapping of qualifications while assuring the inclusion of all training needs.
- Modular character where achievement can be made in small steps and accumulated for gaining recognizable qualification.
- Quality Assurance regime that would promote the portability of skills and labour market mobility.

• Lifelong learning through an improved skill recognition system; recognition of prior learning whether in formal, non-formal or informal arrangements. • Open and flexible system which will permit competent individuals to accumulate their knowledge and skill through testing & certification into higher diploma and degree. • Different learning pathways – academic and vocational – that integrate formal and non-formal learning, notably learning in the workplace, and that offer vertical mobility from vocational to academic learning. • Guidance for individuals in their choice of training and career planning. • Comparability of general educational and vocational qualifications at appropriate levels • Nationally agreed framework of affiliation and accreditation of institutions. 1.1.6 ICT FOR SKILL DEVELOPMENT IN INDIA According to MHRD the Information and Communication Technology (ICT) in schools have been subsumed in the Rashtriya Madhyamik Shiksha Abhiyan (RMSA). Now ICT in Schools is a component of the RMSA. The Information and Communication Technology (ICT) in Schools was launched in December, 2004 and revised in 2010 to provide opportunities to secondary stage students to mainly build their capacity on ICT skills and make them learn through computer aided learning process. The Scheme is a major catalyst to bridge the digital divide amongst students of various socio economic and other geographical barriers. The Scheme provides support to States/UTs to establish computer labs on sustainable basis. Components The scheme has essentially four components:- 1. Partnership with State Government and Union Territories Administrations for providing computer aided education to Secondary and Higher Secondary Government and Government aided schools. 2. Establishment of smart schools, which shall be technology demonstrators. 3. Teacher related interventions, such as provision for engagement of an exclusive teacher, capacity enhancement of all teachers in ICT and a scheme for national ICT award as a means of motivation. 4. Development of e-content, mainly through Central Institute of Education Technologies (CIET), six State Institutes of Education Technologies (SIETs) and Regional Institutes of Education (RIEs), as also through outsourcing. According to National Policy on Information and Communication Technology (ICT) in School Education (2012) ICT will be developed and established for students of the vocational stream at the higher secondary level by integrating them with the need of ICT enabled institutions in the neighbourhood. The scope of these courses would be ICT literacy. It will not be limited to ICT based occupations, but will inform and enhance productivities in a wide range of other occupations. This will also include courses on cyber security. ICT has become an important component of education of many nations. In some schools ICT is taught as a subject and for the majority ICT is a teaching tool. ICT can do wonders in classroom if used wisely by well-trained teachers. ICT enhances teaching and learning process by increasing students' motivation. The use of ICT in classroom helps in the explanation of difficult concepts so students' are able to easily understand those concepts. The integration of ICT in education can takes several forms such as information and computer networks, digital content, internet sites, multimedia and others.

1.1.6 ICT MISSION

ICT integration can be defined as ICT use in classroom teaching (Lloyd, 2005). To build a pervasive ICT environment where learners are guided by ethics, are empowered through the effective use of ICT to prepare them for the current and future world.

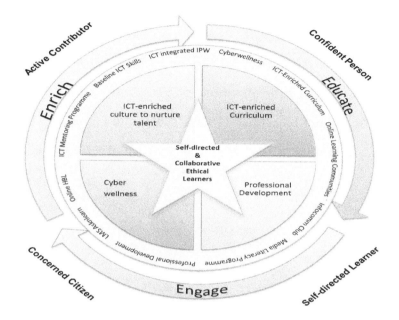

Fig 1.2 ICT framework

1.2   Source: http://www.xingnanpri.moe.edu.sg The States will draw up a Programme of action to inform and guide various aspects of the ICT programme, viz., development of infrastructure, management of the programme, and development of digital resources, capacity building, monitoring and evaluation of the programme. The States' Department of Education will spearhead an advisory group to guide the implementation of the ICT programme, its monitoring and evaluation. The advisory group will consist of the concerned Departments, a reputed engineering Institute of the State, University Departments, etc taking into consideration the variety of technical, educational, financial and administrative tasks involved.

1.3 COMPUTER SELF EFFICACY

Computer has made dramatic effect on our society, especially in the field of education. Computers are common tool in school these days. Although some students are enthusiastic about use of computers, others may be most apprehensive. According to Ertmer (1994), successful computer experience prepares students to participate in a computer dominated society. Computer knowledge and attitudes towards computers also play an important role. Attitude towards computer technologies are associated with a concept of computer self efficacy(Delcourt and Kenzie, 1993), which , in turn has proven to be a factor in in understanding the frequency and success with which individuals use computers(Bandura,1986). The concept of self-efficacy lies at the centre of psychologist Albert Bandura's social cognitive theory. Bandura's theory emphasizes the role of observational learning, social experience, and reciprocal determinism in the development of personality. Compeau and Higgins (1995) defined computer self efficacy as "a judgment of one's capability to use a computer. Computer self efficacy has a major impact on an individual expectation using computers." According to Bandura (1986), self-efficacy can be a better predictor of performance than actual capability because self-percepts are instrumental in determining what individuals do with the knowledge and skills they possess. In his seminal articles, Bandura (1978) identified self-efficacy as a construct often used to explain one's ability to judge how well he/she can execute a task to achieve a desired goal. This was further refined where Bandura highlighted the importance of distinguishing between component skills and the ability to perform actions. To this end, further clarification was offered by other researchers emphasizing that the self efficacy is a person's belief in his/her capability to perform specific tasks and it consists of three dimensions: magnitude, strength and generality: (A) Magnitude – the level of task difficulty an individual believes that he or she can attain, (B) Strength – the confidence one has in attaining a particular level of difficulty and (C) Generality – the degree to which the expectation is generalized across situations. To expand the four origins that affect self-potency thought by Bandura (1986), to explain those four originate computer self-efficacy as follows: 1. Bootstrapping skill: Successful of using computer may result in higher computer self-efficacy, this point is especially important to a new user of computer software. If the new user lacks training of actual operation before the official using of software, the user must suffer the setback when using it Computer self-efficacy is also influenced by the attacked confidence and reduced along with it. 2. Behavior imitation: To study from observing others' behavior performance. Their research discovered that the behavior imitation used as a method in computer training may truly promote the learning of computer self-efficacy and strengthen the training content. 3. The sociality convinces: To guarantee to the users that they have ability to know the computer new science and technology and moreover be able to use it successfully, might help the user to establish the confidence. 4. Physiological condition: People frequently have the anxious feeling because of lack of ability. If a person has the anxious feeling while using the computer and attributes the anxious to insufficient ability; such ideas will reduce their computer self-efficacy. According to Albert Bandura in his Social Learning Theory (1977) "Learning would be exceedingly laborious, not to mention hazardous, if people had to rely solely on the effects of their own actions to inform them what to do. Fortunately, most human behavior is learned observationally through modelling: from observing others one forms an idea of how new behaviours are performed, and on later occasions this coded information serves as a guide for action."

1.2.1 TEACHERS, TECHNOLOLGY AND COMPUTER SELF-EFFICACY

As the pedagogical effectiveness of using computers is widely recognized, all teachers are expected to use them as teaching and learning tools in their classrooms. To do this, however, teachers themselves should be willing to use them. Different studies investigating the relationship between teachers' use of computer technologies and different variables such as self-efficacy beliefs, attitudes towards and knowledge about computer technologies, perceptions of computers as educational tools have revealed that there is a significant correlation between all these variables (Koç, 2005). In other words, the acceptance of computers and their use in the teaching and learning processes as a tool is largely determined by the beliefs, perceptions, and attitudes of teachers (Bitner and Bitner, 2002; Aşkar and Umay, 2001; Milbrath and Kinzie, 2000; Albion, 1999). Therefore, not only should all these psychological constructs be investigated closely but also ways to improve them should be sought.

However, to develop such self-efficacy, teachers need to be introduced to computer technologies systematically and be engaged in activities that will provide them with positive experiences with regard to computer use (Valanides and Angeli, 2008). In this context, self-efficacy beliefs appear to forecast the likely use of computers by pre- service teachers in their future work settings, since people's beliefs about their capabilities are so central and pervasive in human action (Bandura, 1989). Oliver and Shapiro (1993) said that a "individual who did not see himself or herself as a good user were less likely to use computers. If an individual feels comfortable himself or herself toward the computer, it could be said that the individual is ready to use computer or to deal with computer in a specified context."

1.3 SELF REGULATION

Self regulated learning is fairly new construct in research on student's performance and achievement in classroom setting. Both self regulation and self regulated learning can be interchangeably used in educational context as they have same meaning. According to Cook (2014) self regulation is the ability to monitor and control our own behaviour, emotions, thought, altering them in accordance with the demands of situation. It includes the abilities to inhibit first responses, to resist interference from irrelevant stimulation and to persist on relevant task even when it does not enjoy. The term Self-regulation is originally derived from psychology and first defined by Bandura (1988) in terms of three forms of cognitive motivators including causal attributions, outcome expectancies, and cognized goals, each of which is based on its corresponding theory. Zimmerman (1989) defined Self regulation as an integrated learning process, consisting of constructive behaviour that affects one's learning. These planned are adapted to support the pursuit of personal goals in changing learning environment. The self regulation skills can be taught, learned and controlled. Zimmerman (2000) "Self-regulation is the process in which students activate, take control of and evaluate their own learning. Self-regulation is not the same as motivation. Although motivation and self-regulation share some common elements, there are some critical differences. In motivation, choice does not have to be central to the construct. Self-regulation, however, requires some degree of choice or intentional selection of strategies designed to help the learner achieve a goal or behaviour."

1.3.1 DIMENSIONS OF SELF-REGULATION

Zimmerman et al (2002) identified three critical dimensions, or characteristics, of self-regulation:

1. Self observation refers to the willing observation of one's activities. Self observation may take the form of recording frequency, duration or quality of behaviour. Self observation regulates the performance. Self observation can lead to higher motivation.

2. A second critical dimension of self regulation is self adjustment. Self judgement refers to evaluate the student's individual current performance level as compared to the goal level.

3. The third dimension is self reaction. Self reaction refers to one's, behavioural cognitive and affective responses to self judgement.

Self reaction may be motivating if an individual believes they are making progress toward goal.

1.3.2 SELF-REGULATION CYCLE

Self-regulation is a cyclical process because during the process of self-evaluation and monitoring, the learner will make alterations to strategies, cognition and behaviours that will the alter learning and ultimately, the end-goal. (Zimmerman, 2002) There are three phases of the self-regulation cycle are:

1. Forethought is the first phase of self regulation cycle. This phase refers to the processes that set up the learner for action toward their goal. This phase helps the learner to establish a positive outlook, set realistic expectations and address questions such as: 'When will the work start?

2. Performance control is the second phase of self regulation cycle. This phase involves processes that occur during learning that affect action and attention. Specific strategies are established during this stage in order to help a learner to be successful.

3. Self-reflection phase is the third phase of self regulation cycle. During this stage, learners reflect on their performance. According Bandura (1998), Self-regulated learning (SRL) is learning that is guided by Meta cognition (thinking about one's thinking), strategic action (planning

1.1 monitoring, and evaluating personal progress against a standard), and motivation to learn. For Paris and Paris (2001) "Self-regulated learning emphasizes autonomy and control by the individual who monitors, directs, and regulates actions toward goals of information acquisition, expanding expertise, and self-improvement". In particular, self-regulated learners are cognizant of their academic strengths and weaknesses, and they have a repertoire of strategies they appropriately apply to tackle the day-to-day challenges of academic tasks. These learners hold incremental beliefs about intelligence and attribute their successes or failures to factors within their control (Dweck & Leggett, 1988; Dweck, 2002). Finally, students who are self-regulated learners believe that opportunities to take on challenging tasks, practice their learning, develop a deep understanding of subject matter, and exert effort that will give rise to academic success (Perry,2006). Self regulated learners are successful because they control their learning environment. They exert this control by directing and regulating their own actions toward their learning goals. Self regulated learning should be used in three different phases of learning. The first phase is during the initial learning, the second phase is when troubleshooting a problem encountered during learning and the third phase is when they are trying to teach others (Palincsar & Brown, 1984). According to Barry Zimmerman (1989) "Self-regulated learning involves the regulation of three general aspects of academic learning." First, self-regulation of behaviour involves the active control of the various resources students have available to them, such as their time, their study environment (e.g., the place in which they study), and their use of others such as peers and faculty members to help them (Garcia & Pintrich, 1994; Pintrich, Smith, Garcia, & McKeachie, 1993). Second, self-regulation of motivation and affect involves controlling and changing motivational beliefs such as self-efficacy and goal orientation, so that students can adapt to the demands of a course. In addition, students can learn how to control their emotions and affect (such as anxiety) in ways that improve their learning. Third and finally, self-regulation of cognition involves the control of various cognitive strategies for learning, such as the use of deep processing strategies that result in better learning and performance that students showed previously (Garcia & Pintrich, 1994; Pintrich, Smith, Garcia, & McKeachie, 1993). 1.3.1 Common Self-Regulation Strategies Self regulated strategies are an important aspect of self-regulated learning which involves a repertoire of strategies: for learning, studying, controlling emotions, pursuing goals, and so forth. Paris and Winograd (1998) stated , however, it is one thing to know what a strategy is and quite a different thing to be inclined to use and to modify it as task conditions change. Siegle (2005) maintains that the individual set of self-regulation strategies usually used by successful students fall into three categories: personal, these strategies usually involve how a student organizes and interprets information such as goal-setting, planning and monitoring; behavioural, these strategies involve actions that the student takes such as self-evaluating; and environmental, these strategies involve seeking assistance and structuring of the physical study environment, such as seeking information, environmental structuring, and seeking social assistance. The list of strategies as suggested by Siegle (2005) is given below: 1. Personal. These strategies usually involve how a student organizes and interprets information and can include:

1.2 Organizing and transforming information
- outlining
- summarizing
- rearrangement of materials
- highlighting

- flashcards/ index cards
- draw pictures, diagrams, charts
- webs/mapping 1.3 Goal setting and planning/standard setting
- sequencing, timing, completin
- time management and pacing 1.4 Keeping records and monitoring
- note-taking
- lists of errors made

- record of marks
- portfolio, keeping all drafts of assignments

1.3 Rehearsing and memorizing (written or verbal; overt or covert)

- mnemonic devices
- teaching someone else the material
- making sample questions
- using mental imagery
- using repetition

2. Behavioural: These strategies involve actions that the student takes.

2.1 Self-evaluating (checking quality or progress)

- task analysis
- self-instructions; enactive feedback
- attentiveness

2.2 Self Monitoring

- treats to motivate; self-reinforcement
- arrangement or imagination of punishments; delay of gratification

3. Environmental: These strategies involve seeking assistance and structuring of the physical study environment.

3.1 Seeking information (library, Internet)

- library resources

- Internet resources
- reviewing cards
- rereading records, tests, textbooks

3.2 Environmental structuring

- selecting or arranging the physical setting
- isolating/ eliminating or minimizing distractions
- break up study periods and spread them over time

3.3 Seeking social assistance

- from peers
- from teachers or other adults

1.3.2 SOURCES OF SELF-REGULATED LEARNING

1.4 According to Iran-Nejad and Chissom (1992) there are three sources of self-regulated learning: active, dynamic and interest creation. Active self-regulation is regulated by the person and is intentional, conscious, voluntary and strategic. The individual is aware in using such self-regulation strategies. SRL happens best in a habitual mode of functioning. Dynamic self-regulation is also known as unintentional learning because it is regulated by internal subsystems other than the "central executive."The learner is not consciously aware they are learning because it occurs "both under and outside the direct influence of deliberate internal control." The third source of self-regulated learning is the interest-creation. In this model, learning takes place best in a creative mode of functioning and is neither completely person driven nor unconscious, but it is a combination of both. To increase positive attitudes and academic performance, expert learners should be created. Expert learners develop self-regulated learning strategies. One of these strategies is the ability to develop and ask questions and use these questions to expand on their own prior knowledge. This technique allows the learners to test the true understanding of their knowledge and make correction about content areas that have a misunderstanding. When learners engage in questioning, it forces them to be more actively engaged in their learning. It also allows them to self analyze and determine their level of comprehension (Palincsar & Brown, 1984). This active engagement allows the learner to organize concepts into existing schemas. Through the use of questions, learners can accommodate and then assimilate their new knowledge with existing schema. This process allows the learner to solve novel problems and when the existing schema does not work on the novel problem the learner must reevaluate and assess their level of understanding (Paris & Paris, 2001). 1.3.3 Application of self regulation in learning Edirippulige & Marasinghe (2011) reviewed evidences of blending of self-regulated learning with new educational programmes such as e-Health, teaching use of different ICT technologies. There are also many practical applications for self-regulated learning in schools and classrooms today. Paris and Paris (2001) state there are three main areas of direct application in classrooms: literacy instruction, cognitive engagement, and self-assessment. In the area of literacy instruction, educators can teach students the skills necessary to lead them to becoming self-regulated learners by using strategies such as reciprocal teaching, open-ended tasks, and project-based learning. Other tasks that promote self-regulated learning are authentic assessments, autonomy-based assignments, and portfolios. These strategies are student-centred and inquiry based, which cause students to gradually become more autonomous, creating an environment of self-regulated learning. However, students do not simply need to know the strategies, but they need to realize the importance of utilizing them in order to experience academic success. According to Dweck and Master (2008), students who are not self-regulated learners may daydream, rarely complete assignments or forget assignments completely. Those who do practice self-regulation ask questions, take notes, allocate their time effectively, and use resources available to them. These behaviours include, but are not limited to the following: finishing homework assignments by deadlines, studying when there are other interesting things to do, concentrating on school subjects, taking useful class notes of class instruction, using the library for information for class assignments, effectively planning schoolwork, effectively organizing schoolwork, remembering information presented in class and textbooks, arranging a place to study at home without distractions, motivating oneself to do schoolwork, and participating in class discussions. Examples of self regulated learning strategies in practice: Self-Assessment: fosters planning, assess what skills the learner has and what skills are needed. It allows students to internalize standards of learning so that they can regulate their own learning (Laskey &

Hetzel, 2010). Wrapper Activity: activity based on assessment task. This can be done as a homework assignment. It is consists of self-assessment questions to complete before completing homework and then after completion of homework. This will surely help the learner to draw their own conclusions about the learning process (Laskey & Hetzel, 2010). Think Aloud: This involves the teacher describing their thought process in solving a problem (Joseph, 2010). Questioning: student develops questions about the material (Joseph, 2010). Reciprocal Teaching: the learner teaches new material to classmate (Joseph, 2010).

1.5 TECHNOLOGY INTEGRATION BELIEFS

As an international phenomenon, technology is a important part of everybody's lives and efforts to improve teaching and learning (Ammon & Gearhart, 2004). With the importance of technology in education, technology integration has been greatly emphasized in teacher training and professional development (Lawless and Pellegrino, 2007). However, it has been criticized that teachers have not been provided with adequate support (llorens and Grau, 2002). The technology integration is the use of technology tools in general content areas in education in order to allow students to apply computer and technology skills to learning and problem solving. Generally speaking, the curriculum drives the use of technology and not vice versa. According to Dockstader (2008) Technology integration is defined as the use of technology to enhance and support the educational environment. Technology integration in the classroom also supports instruction by creating opportunities for students to complete assignments on the computer rather than the normal pencil and paper. It also helps students to explore more. "Curriculum integration with the use of technology involves the infusion of technology as a tool to enhance the learning in a content area or multidisciplinary setting. Effective integration of technology is achieved when students are able to select technology tools to help them obtain information in a timely manner, analyze and synthesize the information and present it professionally." According to Southeast and island regional technology in education Consortium (1998) leadership is the single most important factor affecting the successful integration of technology. This is true at state level. Schools which have made the most progress are those with energetic and committed leaders. Teachers use technology in two ways. The first way is where technology is used to attain the same traditional goals under the same conditions, without significant change to the classroom activities. The second way to use technology to expand classroom boundaries, connect student to real world events and guide students to become independent learners.

The teacher's use of technology is influenced by the beliefs about teaching and learning (Tubin, 2006). A study was conducted on student's teacher's beliefs about teaching-learning and technology use and found a positive and strong correlation between teachers belief in constructivist teaching and constructivist use of technology (Teo, 2008). Teachers are generally open minded about integrating technology into their teaching but it has been observed that their technology adoption is slow and below expectation (Zhao and Frank, 2003). However, Ertmer (2005) stated that teacher's attitude toward computer use influence the use of technology in classroom. He examined personal factors such as teacher's beliefs that affect technology use in teaching. In other words teachers' beliefs about their ability to use technology play an important role in shaping their responses to instructional reforms, including technology integration for teaching and learning (Selwyn et al, 2001).

1.4.1 TEACHERS BELIEFS IN RELATION TO TECHNOLOGY INTEGRATION

Teachers cannot escape the fact that today's classroom must provide technology supported learning. The international society for technology education report states that today's classroom must empower students with the advantages technology can bring. Teachers should encourage students to become critical thinkers and technology literate citizen. (Sage,2001). Teacher's beliefs are considered an indicator for certain behaviour in classroom because of the mediating effect of beliefs on the ways of teaching via their impact on decision making (Kagan, 1992; Pajares, 1992; William, 2010). According to Hermans et al (2008) "Belief systems consist of an eclectic mix of rules of thumb, generalizations, opinions, values, and expectations grouped in a more or less structured way". Technology integration involves perceptions associated with technology use. Therefore, teacher pedagogical beliefs about technology integration influence teaching methods while using technology. In other words, teachers using technology during instruction depends on pedagogical beliefs to practice. Large amounts of information from numerous sources may confuse students. Thus, teachers need to design learner centred actions that engage students while processing knowledge and foster the ability to think critically about information. Traditional lecture based teaching does not always help students to comprehend complex

1.6   information. As stated, teacher beliefs affect teaching activities. Moreover, constructivist beliefs are positively correlated with the use of technology in the classroom, whereas traditional beliefs are negatively correlated with technology use in the classroom (Hermans et al., 2008). Another definition of beliefs is presented by Alexander and Docahy (1995) who define "beliefs being part of level of perception rather than consisting knowledge or being part of tangible reality." Pajares (1992) stated that one of the most common distinctions between beliefs and knowledge is that beliefs are associated with subjectivity and emotions, whereas knowledge tends to be more empirical. Rokeach (1968) beliefs model consists of the following four main elements: • Existential versus Non-existential beliefs: Those beliefs that are related to existence in physical and social world. • Shared versus unshared beliefs: those beliefs related to share with others. • Derived versus Un-derived beliefs: those beliefs that are not from direct encounter with a particular object. • Beliefs concerning matter of taste: those beliefs that represent matter of choice in an arbitrary way. Consequently, Rokeach(1968) stated that existential vs. non-existential, and shared and unshared beliefs are those having functional connections and consequences on other beliefs. One major difference noted in research on teacher beliefs in technology integration contexts is that the view on beliefs is narrower than in research on teacher technology integration beliefs in general. In other words, it appears that researchers examined beliefs only associated with technology. But truth is that beliefs are associated with teacher beliefs in relation to technology. For example: A teacher believes that the value of technology for student learning is high because a interactive whiteboard allows him to promote active participation in classroom. In contrast, another teacher believes that the value of technology for student learning is high because an interactive whiteboard allows him to deliver content more efficiently by projecting online resources on the board. Although both teachers perceive the value of interactive whiteboard technology to be equally high, their beliefs about the value of the technology do not explain their different uses of that technology. In order to understand why technology is integrated differently among teachers, their fundamental beliefs about what is important in student learning and thus teaching should be understood. Judson (2006) in general teacher with more traditional beliefs will implement more traditional and low level technology uses, whereas teachers with more constructivist beliefs will implement more student centred or high level technology uses.

1.7 COURSE OUTCOMES

The assessment literature is full of terminology such as mission, goals, objectives, outcomes etc. But there is no precise meaning of each of these terms. The outcomes

pyramid shown below presents a pictorial clarification of the hierarchical relationships among different kinds of goals, objectives, and outcomes that appear in assessment literature. Fig 1.3: Outcome pyramid for quality centre national accreditation committee Source: Based on UCF Academic Program Assessment Handbook, 2005 Learning Outcomes are statements that describe significant and essential learning that learners have achieved, and can reliably demonstrate at the end of a course or program. Learning Outcomes identify what the learner will know and able to do by the end of a course or program. Outcomes are achieved results and consequences of what was learned. Learning outcomes on the other hand are more student centred and describes what it is that the learner learnt. According to Reichgelt & Yaverbaum (2002) Course learning outcomes should specify the minimum acceptable standard for a student to be able to pass a course.

This means that it is important to express learning outcomes in terms of the essential learning for a course, so a small number of learning outcomes of central importance should be developed rather than a large number of superficial outcomes. Learning outcomes should be written using action verbs so that students are able to demonstrate that they have learned or achieved the outcome. According to Biggs and Tang (2007) teaching activities should be driven by course learning outcome and should support students in their learning activities and prepare them for assessment. This alignment between learning outcome, learning and teaching methods, assessment criteria makes the whole process transparent to the students. Spady (1994) an educational researcher who spearheaded the development of outcomes based education, suggested that the ability to demonstrate learning is the key point. That demonstration of learning involves a performance of some kind in order to show significant learning that matters. He claims that significant content is essential, but that content alone is insufficient as an outcome. University of Exeter (2007) "programme outcome are related to the qualification level and will relate to the sum of the experience of learners on a particular programme." According to Adam (2004) "learning outcomes are concerned with achievement of learner rather than the intentions of the teachers." With the improvement of web based technology, online learning and computer assisted instruction has become an increasing educational trend (Arbaugh, 2000; Jung & Rha, 2000; Arbaugh & Duray, 2002; Kim, 2004; Lim et al., 2006). Frick, Chadha, Watson, Wang, and Green (2009) pointed out that a course is an instructional product. Therefore, with the increasing number of web-based courses offered in the market, how to choose effective and satisfactory online courses has become an important issue (Mark et al., 2005). Kirkpatrick and Kirkpatrick (1994) stated four levels of evaluation to check the effectiveness of instructional program: (1) Learner's satisfaction (2) Learning (3) Transfer of learning (4) Overall impact on the learner.

These criteria have been widely used in non-formal educational settings (Frick et al., 2009). Frick et al. used the first two criteria, satisfaction and performance, as the indices for evaluating the overall teaching and learning quality in college courses. They found that students' satisfaction and perceived learning were strongly correlated with the global course ratings.

Similarly, Lim et al. (2006) also recommended that course outcomes can be an index for evaluating the overall quality

of distance learning programs. Course outcomes include both cognitive and affective variables (Paechter et al., 2010). Among the cognitive variables. Fig. 1.4: Inverted assessment pyramid (Source: UCF Academic Program handbook, 2005)Fig: 1.4 shows inverted assessment from broad to narrow learning objectives. Goals are not measurable while outcomes are measurable. So while making learning outcome it should be kept in mind. Learning achievement is the most important one, whereas course satisfaction is the important affective variable (Lim et al. 2006) Paechter et al., 2010 e illustrate the different ways in which the term student outcome can be used: • Positive and negative outcomes: Generally speaking, student outcomes are considered—either explicitly or implicitly—to be positive or negative by educators. If students are learning what they are expected to learn, or graduation rates in a school are rising, these results would generally be viewed as "positive student outcomes." Conversely, low or declining test scores and high dropout rates would be "negative student outcomes." Instructional outcomes: Schools and teachers may define student outcomes as the knowledge, skills, and habits of work that students are expected to acquire by the end of an instructional period, such as a course, program, or school year. Teachers often establish Instructional goals for a course, project, or other learning experiences and those goals may then be used to guide what and how they teach. Educational outcomes: The results achieved by schools may also be considered "student outcomes" by educators and others, including results such as graduation grades and college-enrolment rates. In this sense, the term may be synonymous with student achievement, since achievement typically implies education-specific results such as improvements in test scores. Societal and life outcomes: In some cases, the term student outcomes, and synonyms such as educational outcomes, may imply broader, more encompassing, and more far-reaching educational results, including the impact that education has on individuals and society. 1.5.1 COURSE SATISFACTION Course Satisfaction is a well researched topic in both academic and non-academic settings. In academic settings, student's satisfaction data helps colleges and universities make their curriculum more responsive to the needs of a changing market place

(Eyck, Tews & Ballester, 2009; Witowski, 2008). The increasing demand and growing students experience with flexible education programs to support career development and lifelong learning has increased student's expectations for quality instruction, effective educational outcome and finally satisfaction for learning (Debourgh, 1999). Allen et al. (2002) and Wang (2003) argued that in any educational institution, the satisfaction of a student can be determined from his level of pleasure as well as the effectiveness of the educational program that the student experiences. Students with higher levels of satisfaction towards various aspects of courses are reported to show considerably higher levels of learning than students with low level of satisfaction (Fredericksen, 2000). According to Selby Markham (2014) the analysis of student's satisfaction with their course and program of study is an important research area within educational evaluation. With the growing concern for accountability in educational outcomes, the need for meaningful and stable measures has grown. He defined "Satisfaction as being a consequence of the expectation and experiences of the subject and course". The Sloan Consortium defines student satisfaction: "Students are successful in the learning experience and are pleased with their experience" (Moore, 2009). Sweeney and Ingram (2001) define student satisfaction as "the perception of enjoyment and accomplishment in the learning environment". "Student satisfaction reflects the effectiveness of all aspects of the educational experience. The goal is that all students who complete a course express satisfaction with course rigor and fairness, with professor and peer interaction, and with support services" (Sloan, 2010) 1.5.2 COMPUTER ACHIEVEMENT Achievement means the amount of knowledge gained by the student in different subjects of study. Knowledge of an individual's achievement helps the teacher to know the effectiveness of teaching methods and also encourages the students to work hard and learn more. The term achievement is synonymous with the accomplishment or proficiency of performance in a given skill or body of knowledge. Hawes and Hawes (1982) defined achievement as successful accomplishment or performance in a particular subjects, area or course, usually by reasons of skills, hard work and interest, typically summarized in various types of grade, marks, scores or descriptive commentary. According to Mehta (1969) was of the view that the word performance is a wider term including academic and co-curricular achievement. According to him achievement is a learning outcome of students' activities in which performance of individual is included. Thus it is a dynamic phenomenon and not static. According to Megargee (2000) achievement tests are how well students mastered the subject matter in a course of instruction. Achievement test is a standardized test that is designed to measure an individual's level of knowledge in a particular area unlike an aptitude test which measures a person's ability to learn something. An achievement test focuses specifically on how much a person knows about a specific topic or area such as math, computer and science (Alley, 1999) Ollendik (2003) defined computer achievement as the knowledge and computer skills that an individual learns through computer instruction. Achievement tests measures what a person has learned. Achievement is measured through achievement test. Achievement test are Direct measures of what they are designed to measure. Achievement test serve many of the same functions as test of general intelligence and special abilities. The purpose of achievement test is to measure some aspects of the intellectual competence of human being: what a person has learned to know or to do. Teachers use achievement test to measure the attainment of their students. Thus, achievement tests measure the extent to which a person has achieved something, acquired certain information, or measured certain skills-usually as result of planned instruction, training and program. It is designed to measure the amount of knowledge and skills a person has acquired as result of classroom instruction. Computer Achievement in the present study will be studied at three categories of bloom's taxonomy of the cognitive domain, viz., knowledge, comprehension and application categories of objectives. Thus it can be summarised that information and communication technology plays a significant role in the field of education. All over the world ICT is used in teaching and learning process. The teacher and student must access to technology for improving learning outcomes. There is rapid shift of educational technologies to shape the structure of education system. In today's society, digital literacy acquires increasing importance for any professional profile. ICT is an effective technique to improve the academic performance and technology integration beliefs of the prospective teacher which is otherwise difficult with the traditional teaching method.

CHAPTER II

REVIEW OF RELATED LITERATURE

Review of the literature is an essential part of the research process. The review of related literature implies locating, analyzing and evaluating findings of relevant researches, study of published articles, going through portions of encyclopaedias and abstracts etc. A review of related literature helps to show whether the evidence already available solves the problem adequately without further investigation and thus to avoid the risk of duplication. Since good research is based upon everything that is known in the area of research, the review of related literature provides a basis for the formulation of hypotheses. The review of related literature helps the researcher to delimit and define her problem, and also to avoid sterile problem areas. Considering the pros and cons of premier research and success of the investigators and educationist in this area, the present study has been forwarded with the review of literature of the main issues discussed, which the investigator could gather with all the resources available at his disposal. There are very sources for data collection which can be classified mainly as primary and secondary:

- Primary Resources- These are direct sources where first hand information can be obtained from the persons with eye-witness account of events, technical experts in the specific fields of study and interaction with experienced persons or objects through the appropriate use of instruments give information in an unmodified manner.
- Secondary Sources – These include published materials such as educational journals, monographs, books, bulletins, government publications, dissertations and theses.
- Other Sources- Encyclopaedias of education, educational journals, educational indexes, educational abstracts, directorates and bibliographies, quotation resources and miscellaneous sources.

In writing the literature review, the purpose is to convey the reader what knowledge and ideas have been established on a topic and what their strength and weaknesses. Some of the researches related to the variables in the study are presented under the following sub- headings:

2.1 Research studies related to ICT skills

2.2 Research studies related to information and communication technology skills development program

2.3 Research studies related to computer self efficacy

2.4 Research studies related to self regulation

2.5 Research studies related to technology integration and beliefs

2.6 Research studies related to courses outcomes

2.1 RESEARCH STUDIES RELATED TO ICT SKILLS

Beyerbach (2001) found a significant increase in technology integration for both pre- service and in-service teacher after participation in a preparation course. After completion of course, teachers were able to incorporate a constructivist view of technology integration into their instruction in order to engage students in meaningful learning. The pre-service teachers reported great benefits from the use of technology in the classroom after the course. The study concluded that simply teaching basic ICT skills is inadequate if teachers are not able to integrate technology constructively into their instruction. More emphasis should be placed on advanced skills in teacher education programs in order to provide teachers with authentic opportunities to experience and develop lessons that integrate technology in a meaningful context. The finding also encourage collaboration in learning in technology related assignments.

Hakkarainen et al. (2001) investigated the relationship between ICT, pedagogical thinking and self reported practices. 600 questionnaires were distributed among the elementary and high school teachers. The study indicated that only a small percentage of teachers had adequate ICT skills. The study also reported that teachers, who actively used computer in classroom, emphasized the importance of using ICT and collaborative learning. Further, the results found that the discrepancy between teachers' pedagogical thinking that commonly emphasized active construction of knowledge and self-reported pedagogical practices was lower for teachers who intensively use ICT as compared with teachers who do not use ICT in classroom.

Doering, Hughes and Huffman (2003) investigated the perspective regarding the ICT in future classroom of pre-service teachers before and after participation in teacher preparation program. Before the preparation course, teachers were doubtful about the utility of ICT in the classroom. Significant difference was found in their perspective regarding ICT after the completion of course. Their doubt had transformed into positive sentiment. They found that technology can assist in learning and to recognize its importance.

Terry, Lewer and Macy (2003) conducted an instructional program on 240 students in the three formats of online, on-campus and hybrid. Using a standard regression model where final exam score is the dependent variable and student characteristics are the independent variables. They found that predicted exam scores for students in the online courses were significantly less than those of students in the on-campus and in the hybrid formats. However, there was no significant difference between the exam scores of students in the hybrid and on campus classes.

Bunz et al. (2007) investigated general investigated general operating system skills, email and web skills asking respondents how much thought the listed activities would require. Result revealed that less computer anxiety reported. However, there was no significant relationship found between computer anxiety and actual fluency. They also found no gender difference as to actual CEW fluency, but women perceived their fluency lower than did men.

Chai, Koh and Tsai (2010) investigated pre-service teacher's beliefs about the use of computer technology and the effectiveness of ICT courses. The results indicated that after participating in courses, pre-service teachers recognized the importance of technology integration into their curricula and believed that ICT use would enhance student learning. They felt that need of such courses prepared them to apply ICT in the future, and their abilities to select, evaluate, and use a variety of technological resources improved. They found that ICT courses through the technology enhanced lesson (TEL) approach helped teachers learn how to use technologies as supporting tools in order to enhance their teaching and student learning.

Alazam et.al (2012) studied the levels of ICT usage in the classroom among technical and vocational teachers in Malaysia. Three hundred twenty nine questionnaires were distributed among the technical and vocational teachers who were teaching engineering subject in Malaysian technical and vocational schools. The questionnaire had items related to teacher's ICT skills, ICT use and their demographic factors. The study had found that teacher's ICT skills were at moderate levels. There were significant differences found in teacher's ICT skills as a function of demographic factors: gender, age, years of teaching experience, and type of ICT training. Study revealed significant correlations found between ICT skills and ICT integration in classroom. Results showed that Teacher's demographic factors did not influence ICT integration in classroom.

Ng (2012) surveyed the demand for various ICT skills by ascertaining the perceived value of these skills to organisations in both the short and longer time. In total, 590 questionnaires were distributed to the organisations, randomly selected from compass Database via Massy University 'website with 100 or more employees nationwide. The research finding revealed that, in both the short and longer, there is moderate to high demand for the majority of skills examined in this study. The top three skills that were rated as being the most valuable in both the short and longer term are managing the ICT function Application support, IT operation network operation & network support. The skills that were positively related to technological specialties are in higher demand in the short term than the non-technological skills were seen as being more important than the direct technological skills in the longer term.

Callum & Jeffery 2013 determined how ICT skills impact student's adoption of mobile learning. The study revealed that the perceived ease of use and usefulness of mobile technology would mediate the relationship between ICT skills and the intention of student to adopt mobile learning. A survey of 446 students from three tertiary institutions found that student's intention to adopt mobile learning was influenced by specific types of ICT skills. It was found that advanced skill in mobile technology and basic ICT skills both played significant roles in the intention to adopt mobile learning.

Umar et al. (2014) investigated the correlation among teacher's years of service, computer experience and effects of ICT on teaching and learning. A set of 7320 questionnaire had been mailed to primary and secondary school teachers throughout Malaysia. There was no correlation found between the teacher's years of service and perceived impact of ICT on their teaching and student learning. A weak correlation was found between computer experience and impact of ICT on teaching. There was no correlation between the respondent's computer experience and the impact of ICT on student learning. Furthermore, the findings indicated that the male teachers use

ICT in classroom significantly more frequently than their female colleagues for teaching and learning as well as for creating presentation materials.

2.1.1 Trend analysis

The trend analysis shows that ICT skills enhance the achievement level , Impacts teacher's adoption, helps in integration of technology in classroom and effect psychomotor behavior of the students as well as pre service and prospective teachers . Beyerbach (2001) found a significant increase in technology integration for both pre service and in – service teacher after participation in a preparation course. Alazam, Bakar, Hamzah & Asmiran (2012) found significant correlations between ICT integration in classroom. Teacher's demographic factors (age, gender, teaching experience, except level of education) did not influence ICT integration in classroom. On the country, Umar, & Yusoff (2014) found no correlation between the teacher's years of service and impact of ICT on their teaching. Eyitayo (2012) provides a conceptual framework for individuals; organisations and information system community to be able to study the skills needs, as well as develop appropriate ICT information resources that will meet the needs of the target group.

2.2 RESEARCH STUDIES RELATED TO INFORMATION AND COMMUNICATION TECHNOLOGY SKILLS DEVELOPMENT PROGRAM

Montignty & Rondeau (2001) investigated teacher's self efficacy and beliefs with regard to ICT use in an online program. Before the online computer program respondents felt they had mastered all basic ICT skills, with the exception of antivirus software and participation in group discussion. After the program respondents learnt new skills, particularly when the introduction of new innovations for teaching and learning was introduced through online program. Significant difference was found in their self efficacy and beliefs after the online program. They concluded that their ICT self-efficacy, ICT skills and learning requirements had increased after the appropriate program.

Jarmo (2001) found that the incorporation of ICTs into the TVE programs in schools provided good opportunities for students to communicate with the world of work not just outside the school but also around the world. In fact, the integration of ICT in TVE programs enabled students and teachers to explore the world of work with ease and made teaching and learning more meaningful.

Brown and Liedholm (2002) investigated the difference in students taught through online program and face-to face by the same teacher. They found significant difference in the exam scores of both group. The students who were taught on-campus format got higher scores than students who were taught through online format. They reported the relatively better performance in the on-campus classes to the benefit of in-person teacher-student interactions and attribute the relatively poorer performance of the students in the online class to the lack of self discipline necessary for successful independent learning in the online environment.

Oh & French (2002) studied the importance of the technology standards for the pre service teacher preparation programs and the students perceptions of the adequate use of technology for their teaching practices. The survey was conducted with 80 students who enrolled in the Introductory Instructional Technology Course at a research university in the southeast in fall 2002. Findings revealed that the standard based curriculum and the use of project based assessment enabled students to achieve all the necessary skills and knowledge through cross-curricular hands on practice during the course.

Burdett et al. (2003) investigated the sources of resistance as identified by academic staff in using ICT. The university had provided their staff with encouragement and web tools since 1999. All courses were provided with an automatically generated web-page, but the implementation of ICT for teaching and learning was optional. Burdett interviewed ten academics, split between early and late adopters. Result revealed that early adopters were using ICT at higher levels than late adopter. It was also discovered that early adopter utilises several features of webpage such as quiz and online discussion than late adopters,, who tend to not use the web page at all. Early adopters were more interested in using new and innovative technologies and believed there was potential for ICT to improve learning.

Zavaraki (2003) performed a study on the use of network communications in academic transactions by teachers and its impact on learning outcomes of post graduate students in India. This study was conducted on 260 university teachers and 500 post graduate students of faculty of Science, Social Science and commerce, Panjab University, Chandigarh. He compared user and non-user faculty and their students in their attitude towards network communication, the findings revealed that user faculty teachers had more positive attitude towards internet in higher education as compared to non-user faculty teachers. In addition, post graduate students belonging to user faculty teachers had more positive attitude towards internet technology and more general information about computers (MS word, MS Excel, Power Point) as compared to students who belonged to non-user faculty teachers.

Sosin et al. (2004) studied the impact of ICT program on the academic performance of the students. Data were collected from 3,986 students, taught by 30 instructors in 15 institutions in the United States of America during the spring and autumn semesters of 2002. They found significant and low positive impact on student performance due to ICT use. Results showed that some ICT skills seem to be positively correlated to performance while others are not.

Fuchs & Woessman (2004) conducted a study to find correlation between the availability of ICT and students performance. The analysis of the effects of these methodological and technological innovations on the students attitude towards the learning process and on students' performance seems to be evolving towards a consensus, according to which an appropriate use of digital technologies in higher education can have significant positive effects both on students' attitude and their achievement. Results revealed strong and significantly positive correlation between the availability of ICT and students performance. They also found small and insignificant correlation when other student environment characteristics are taken into consideration.

Leuven et al. (2004) concluded that there is no evidence for a relationship between increased educational use of ICT and students' performance. In fact, they find a consistently negative and marginally significant relationship between ICT use and some student achievement measures. Students may use ICT to increase their leisure time and have less time to study. He found no relation between on line gaming and increased achievement

Jones & Jones (2005) compared teacher and student attitudes concerning use and effectiveness of web based course. His result identified that attitudes of both faculty and students were positive. Both believed that the World Wide Web was a beneficial e-learning tool in teaching learning process. They considered themselves computer

literate, active and competent course into users. Result revealed that faculty has significantly high correlation than students.

Lim & Khine (2006) examined the strategies employed by four Singapore schools in order to manage barriers in and out of the classroom to ICT implementation. They found six operating strategic elements, based on the observation of ICT lessons and face-to-face interviews with teachers, directors of ICT and school headmaster. These included: technical support staff; training of students ICT helpers; time for teacher to prepare for ICT; collaboration among teachers; support provided by headmaster in addressing teachers' ICT concerns; training for teachers on how to use ICT in the classroom. They evaluated factors in terms of ICT application by teachers and students and assess the availability and roles of technical support, the training and skill of teacher in ICT and support provided by the headmaster in addressing teachers' ICT concern in schools.

Tanvisuith (2008) examined the influence of self-determined motivation on ICT training outcomes and subsequent ICT acceptance with an emphasis on internet skill development and usage in Thai community technology centres supported by the Microsoft Unlimited Potential grants. The result revealed that the individuals who have higher self determined motivation to participate in ICT training programs are more likely to develop computer self-efficiency, positive training satisfaction and strong usage intention.

Youssef (2008) examined the relationship between the use of information and communication technology (ICT) and student performance in higher education. The paper summarized the main findings and gives two complementary explanations. The first explanation focused on the indirect effects of ICT on standard explanatory factors. ICT had an impact on the outcome of education. The differences observed in students 'performance are thus more related to the differentiated impact of ICT on standard explanatory factors. The second hypothesis advocated that ICT uses need a change in the origination of higher education. Result observed differences in students' achievement.

Goktas et al. (2009) tried to find the main barriers and possible enablers for integrating information and communication technologies (ICTs) in Turkey's pre- service teacher education programs. The data were collected by questionnaires from

53 deans in schools of teacher education (STE), 111 teacher educators and 1,330 prospective teachers and additionally from interviews of six teacher educators and six prospective teachers. The findings indicated that the majority of the stakeholders believed that lack of in-service training, lack of appropriate software and materials and lack of hardware are the main barriers for integrating ICTs in pre-service teacher education programs.

Barkhuizene (2010) conducted an exploratory, ex post facto study on soft skills and technical skills. Retention surveys were administered among a purposive sample of 79 graduate interns and 39 mentors in a South African ICT company. Both groups of participants indicated that the soft skills presented in the training are important. Results showed that the technical skills training contributed to a large extent to the employability of the graduate intern. Result revealed that Technical skills during training were significantly related to the graduate intern's intention to quit the internship programme.

Ozsevgec (2010) conducted a research on pre-service teacher to find out the relationship between grades and teacher training programs in relation to their computer literacy. Data were collected from 276 pre-service teachers through a case study method. The Computer Literacy Scale having 24 likert-type questions was employed. The inferential statistical tests were used to analyze obtained data for comparing groups on the scores collected from different tests. The research revealed that there was no difference found between grades and senior pre service teachers' computer literacy. Undergraduate programs only have developed basic skills of pre service students and have not had the impact on other skills and computer literacy.

Mwalongo (2011) examined teachers' perceptions about the use of ICT tools for teaching, professional development and personal use. Data were collected from 74 teachers through an online survey. Results indicated that while the frequency of use of ICT was influenced by access, the competence of ICT use was influenced by training. It was found that teachers used ICT in a wide range for teaching, professional development and personal use. However, it was also found teachers did not use ICT to radically change their pedagogical practices, but rather to sustain their traditional practices.

Wanjala & Mukwa (2011) studied the factors that are significant in professional staff development that contribute to the efficacy of secondary school teacher's use of information communication technologies in instruction. A questionnaire survey was developed and used to collect data from secondary schools teachers in Bungoma district of Kenya. A stratified random sampling technique was employed to select samples drawn independently and randomly from the stratum of secondary schools. The results indicated that the few teachers use ICTs to manage the classroom and to integrate technology into several of the content areas. Findings indicated that most teachers use trial and error, learn through course work taken at colleges or universities, and support others or receive personal or expert support as significant methods of learning how to use Information communication technologies.

Nisar et al. (2011) studied impact and usage of ICT in Education sector of Pakistan. Data were accumulated from 429 respondents from five colleges and universities from district Rawalpindi of Pakistan, using convenient sampling method. The result showed that Availability and Usage of ICT improves the knowledge and learning skills of students. This indicated that existence of ICT improved the educational efficiency as well as obliging for making policies regarding education sector.

Vronska (2012) developed a model of ICT integration skills development for the prospective teachers of subjects, Household and Home economics. It was found that if traditional study course is supplemented with the elements of ICT, the student's educational level increases, besides, it increases in proportion with the number of computer programs acquired in the study course. The author concluded that usage of ICT promotes individualization of the study process that depends on the qualification level, skills, peculiarities of acquiring the learning material, student's interests and needs.

Sarkar (2012) investigated the impact of ICT in higher education. It was evident from the study that use of ICT in education increased very rapidly in various states of India. One of the most common problems of using Information and Communication Technologies (ICTs) in education is to base choices on technological possibilities rather than educational needs. The use of ICT in education lends itself to more student-centred learning settings. The study found that the role of ICT in education has become more and more important and this importance will continue to grow and develop.

Sabzwari et al. (2012) investigated the awareness, usage and impact of information and communication technologies (ICTs) for information, education and research purposes among research students of Bahauddin Zakariya University, Multan. Data was collected through questionnaire from students involved in research and analysed. It was found that majority of research students were not aware about using Endnote for preparing bibliographies and organizing citation and SPSS for data analyzing. It was also found that they had inadequate knowledge about HEC digital library. It was also found most of students don't have knowledge of basic skills of computer.

Osakwe & Regina (2013) investigated the impact of Information and Communication Technology (ICT) on teacher education programme and professional development of learners in Nigeria. The data was collected from 206 students of colleges of education, randomly selected using stratified sampling technique. Results revealed that there was significant relationship between ICT and research, effective student learning, access to information materials for teaching and professional development. The results of the hypotheses revealed that there is a significant relationship between ICT and lesson presentation, access to information on teaching materials, student's effective learning and professional development.

Dagiene (2013) investigated the pre-service educational programmes for teachers' ICT competency in Lithuanian universities and colleges. The research was based on "Teachers' Training on ICT Application in Education" developed by the Institute of Mathematics and Informatics in 2009. The study suggested deeper content-based modules for pedagogical ICT competency and skills in all-level pre-service teacher education as well as in-service training courses.

Urama (2014) investigated to find out the level of application of ICT in educational management at the Federal College of Education, Nigeria. Data were collected from staff of the institution through questionnaires. The data from the questionnaires were analyzed and results showed that due to the application of ICT in various operational sections of the institution, there was significant improvement in service delivery and general management of the institution.

Kretschmann (2015) examined the subjective theories of Physical Education (PE) teachers about integrating ICT into PE. Data was collected from 57 in-service secondary school PE teachers through the developed instrument. The data was analyzed using standard statistical techniques. He suggested focus on the subjective theories and their relation to gender, computer literacy, household computer ownership, and professional experience.

2.2.1 Trend Analysis

The trend analysis shows that the impact of ICT on the learning process seems to be more important and requires more than looking only to curricula. Improved student outcomes are observed, with regard to: motivation, enjoying learning; self-esteem; collaborative skills; subject knowledge; information handling skills; meta-cognitive skills. These results have been supported by Osakwe & Regina (2013); Sarkar (2012); Vronska (2012);; Dagiene (2013); Fuchs & Woessman (2004). Mwalongo (2011) examined teachers' perceptions about the use of ICT tools for teaching, administration, professional development and personal use. Results indicated that while the frequency of use of ICT was influenced by access, the competence of ICT use was influenced by training; teachers used ICT in a wide range for teaching, administration, professional development and personal use. However, teachers did not use ICT to radically change their pedagogical practices, but rather to sustain their traditional practices. Alazzam (2012) found no significant effect of teachers' educational background and support factors on teachers' overall ICT readiness. In addition, Fuchs & Woessman (2004) found positive correlation between the availability of ICT and students' attitude and achievement. Sabzwari, Bhatti, & Ahmed, 2012) found most of students don't have knowledge of basic skills of computer. Nisar, Munir & Shad (2011); Wanjala (2011); Mukwa (2011) supported existence of ICT in improving the educational efficiency as well as obliging for making policies regarding education sector.

2.3 RESEARCH STUDIES RELATED TO COMPUTER SELF EFFICACY

Giacquinta (2000) found that educational technology students reported using computers more frequently, for a wider array of purposes and for greater number of hours each week than students in the Educational Administration, Business Education and Higher Education programs. They also reported completing more formal

instruction and more positive attitudes toward the value of computers in academic studies.

Dinev (2002) examined computer self-efficacy and Internet use, including the possible precursors to Internet user anxiety. The author discussed how anxieties that are developed about Internet use can cause aversion using the Internet in general, and especially in using it for unfamiliar applications. He hypothesized that self-efficacy is an important determinant of Internet anxiety. Factor analysis of Dinev's survey of 70 undergraduate students showed that items could be divided into two categories for Internet self-efficacy and use; general (e.g. surfing and emailing) and advanced (e.g. making web pages and discussion boards). There were strong correlations between Internet anxiety factors, self-efficacy factors and the Internet specific factors. Significant correlations were found s between Internet anxiety and Internet specific factors such as technical, intrusion and security concerns.

Piper and Yan (2003) reported a significant influence of self-efficacy on novice teachers' classroom uses of technology based on their survey of 160 elementary and secondary teachers. In fact, evidence suggested that self-efficacy may be more important than skills and knowledge among teachers who implement technology in their class- rooms.

Bauer and Kenton (2005) reported that a greater number of technology-using teachers rated themselves as being highly confident (n=14) for using computer technology, compared to being highly skilled (n=9). In a survey of 764 teachers, he found that one of the two greatest predictors of teachers' technology use was their confidence that they could achieve instructional goals using technology.

Sam, Othman and Nordin (2005) surveyed computer self-efficacy, computer anxiety and attitude towards internet. The findings suggested that the under graduates had moderate computer anxiousness, medium attitudes towards the internet, and high computer self-efficacy and used the Internet extensively for educational purposes such as doing research, downloading electronic resources and e-mail communications. Under graduates with better attitudes towards the internet did more 'downloading of software and games' activities and they had higher computer self-efficacy. It also found a significant relationship between computer anxiety and attitudes towards internet. Undergraduates who are highly computer anxious generally have negative attitudes towards the internet.

Hasan (2005) showed a positive relationship between an individual's computer self-efficacy (CSE) and his/her ability to learn new computing skills. Study focused on two issues by investigating the impact of two levels of CSE (general and software specific) on two types of learning (near- and far-transfer) in computer training. The results of an experiment conducted to empirically test the relationships hypothesised among the study variables showed that software-specific CSE had significant effects on near-transfer and far-transfer learning and software-specific self-efficacy. In contrast, general CSE was found to have a significant effect on far-transfer learning only.

Kurt (2007) determined the level of teachers' computer self-efficacy and whether the computer self-efficacy changes according to their age, gender, owning computer and frequency of computer use. The results indicate that the teachers' level of computer self-efficacy was 71.52, 20-25 aged and 0-5 years experienced teachers' computer self-efficacies were higher than the others. No significant difference was found between gender and teachers' computer self-efficacy. The teachers who had computer and who always used computer had higher computer self-efficacies than the others.

Anderson and Maninger (2007) investigated the changes in and factors related to students' technology-related abilities, beliefs, and intentions. Statistically significant changes were found in students' perceived abilities, self-efficacy beliefs, value beliefs, and intentions to use software in their future classrooms. Students' self-efficacy, value beliefs, and intentions were moderately correlated with each other.

Embi (2007) reported that computer self-efficacy is the best predictor of level of computer anxiety. He found that 36% of the variation in computer anxiety can be explained by the regression model with computer self-efficacy as a single predictor alone. Moreover, an inverse relationship exists between computer anxiety and computer self-efficacy, it indicated that computer self-efficacy is an important factor in determining the accounting faculty levels of computer anxiety and the extent to which computer applications have been used either as a tool to support instruction or taught to students as a part of the course curriculum.

Ocak and Akdemir (2008) investegated science teachers' computer literacy level is related to their computer use. And, also computer literacy level of the teachers increases their integration of computer applications in their teaching. In the study, most of the teachers use Internet, email, and educational software CDs as computer applications in the classrooms. They found statistical differences in the integration of computer applications as an instructional tool.

Liaw (2008) conducted survey on 424 university students using a standard questionnaire. The results showed that perceived self-efficacy is a critical factor that influences learners' satisfaction with the Blackboard e-learning system. Perceived usefulness and perceived satisfaction both contribute to the learners' behavioral intention to use the e-learning system. Furthermore, e-learning effectiveness can be influenced by multimedia instruction, interactive learning activities, and e-learning system quality. This research proposed a conceptual model for understanding learners' satisfaction, behavioral intention, and effectiveness of using the e-learning system.

Penna and Stara's (2009) performed a study in a primary

school, designed to test whether expectations and opinions on computers, both of students and teachers might be related to the effectiveness of computer use within a particular educational context. Findings do not appear to support the hypothesis that a positive opinion on computers can lead to higher learning efficacy in a computer-based educational environment.

Saade and Kira (2009) investigated the influence of computer anxiety on perceived ease of use and the mediating effect of computer self-efficacy on this relationship, within an e-learning context. A survey methodology approach was used to collect data from 645 university students. The psychometric properties of the items and constructs were validated followed by the assessment of mediation of computer self efficacy. Results from the use of a learning management system indicated that computer self- efficacy plays a significant role in mediating the impact of anxiety on perceived ease of use. With the continuous development of richer and more integrated interfaces, anxieties about learning to use the new interface and executing tasks effectively becomes of primary importance.

Laosethakul (2009) found that how computer anxiety and

computer self-efficacy influence gender perception toward computing of Chinese female in comparison to

American female. One of the findings indicated that computer anxiety directly impacts gender perception towards computing of females in both cultures.

Teo (2009) examined the relationship between computer self-efficacy and intended uses of technology of student teachers (N=1094) at a teacher training institute in Singapore. Participants responded to a 7-point Likert-type scale for each factor. Analysis was conducted using the structural equation modelling approach and a good model fit was found for both the measurement and structural models. Results showed that significant relationships exist among Basic Teaching Skills (BTS), Advanced Teaching Skills (ATS), and Technology for Pedagogy (TP), However, ATS did not influence Traditional Use of Technology (TUT) and Constructivist Use of Technology (CUT) in a significant way. Overall, the results of this study offer some evidence that student teachers' self-efficacy is a significant influence on whether they use technology in a traditionalist or constructivist way.

Teo and Koh (2010) examined the computer self-efficacy among 708 pre-service teachers at a teacher training institute in Singapore. Data were collected through self- reported ratings on a 7-point Likert-type scale. The result revealed that pre-service teachers' computer self-efficacy was explained by three factors: Basic Computer Skills (BCS), Media-Related Skills (MRS), and Web-Based Skills (WBS). The result revealed adequate representations of pre-service teachers' computer self-efficacy.

Mehra and Omidian (2010) investigated 'A cross cultural comparison of attitude towards e-learning among Indian and Iranian University students in relation to their computer self-efficacy and anxiety' revealed that out of a sample of 400 Indian students, 79% had their computer self-efficacy levels in confident or very confident category. 14.5% of Indian students moderately agreed that they had confidence about their beginning skills, 42.3% had a strong confidence about their file and software skills. Students from the science faculty were more confident with use of computer as compared to arts/education faculty. A positive relationship was found between attitudes towards e-learning and computer self-efficacy, and a negative correlation was found between computer self-efficacy and computer anxiety. Computer self-efficacy had a significant positive effect on total scores of students' attitudes towards e-learning.

Alenezi et al. (2010) investigated the role of enjoyment, computer anxiety, computer self-efficacy and Internet experience in influencing the students' intention to use E-learning in Saudi's universities. 402 governmental universities' students participated in the study to test the proposed hypotheses and to determine whether the proposed variables have an effect on the students' intention to use E-learning system. The results of stepwise regression indicated that computer anxiety, computer self-efficacy and enjoyment significantly influence the students' intention to use E-learning.

Caroline Farah (2011) examined factors influencing teachers' levels of technology self-efficacy through a qualitative multi-site, multi-subject case study research design. An initial survey was administered to all full-time, certified teachers at three school sites in order to gauge teacher's current level of technology self-efficacy. From that population, purposive and systematic sampling was used to draw the participants for the case study. A group of nine teachers with varying levels of technology self- efficacy was interviewed and participated in one of three focus groups to better understand factors influencing their current level of self-efficacy. A document analysis was also performed of local school professional development plans. Results revealed several factors that influenced teachers technology self-efficacy, including personal, behavioral, and environmental factors.

Adalıer (2012) revealed the relation between 136 Turkish and English language teacher candidates' perceived computer self-efficacy and attitudes toward computer at the universities in Cyprus. He found that there is a medium level positive statistical difference between perceived computer self-efficacy and attitudes toward computer.

Tantrarungroj & Suwannatthachote (2012) investigated pre-service teachers' self- efficacy in designing digital media and their technological pedagogical content knowledge (TPCK) for designing digital media using different forms of self-regulated learning instructional support for online project-based learning. The study used a 2 × 2 factorial research design. The sample consisted of 232 pre-service teachers from an institution situated in Bangkok, Thailand. Two-way Multivariate Analysis of Variance (MANOVA) was used for data analysis. The results showed significant differences in pre-service teachers' self-efficacy and TPCK post test scores.

No main effect was found between two different self-regulated learning strategies (SQ and PA) upon the means of self-efficacy in designing digital media scores and TPCK scores.

Poelmans, Truyen & Stockman (2012) focused on several students' perceived ICT skills, general computer use patterns and perceived computer self-efficacy. Sample consisted of 195 students at bachelor and master level. It was scored on 6 dimensions within global ICT skills: File Management, Security, Technical Issues, Legal Issues, Internet and Awareness and compared this to computer self-efficacy levels. Existence of gender effects, bachelor-master effects and the impact of the chosen study subject and computer use were investigated. The results showed that students in the sample rate their own ICT skills quite high, apart from the dimensions, legal and technical issues. It was found that specific computer use profiles, such as identifying oneself as a 'blogger', renders good self-efficacy predictions. While the gender and study subject effects are limited, significant differences between master and bachelor students have been revealed.

Gencturk (2013) studied the technological self-efficacy of primary school teachers, and compared their technological efficiencies depending on gender and professional experience variables. The study was quantitative descriptive and survey method was applied to collect data. The data of the study was gathered through personal information questionnaire and "Technology Self-Efficacy Scale". The results of the research showed that technology self-efficacy beliefs of teacher were in the mid level. In addition, it was found that while technology self-efficacy beliefs of teachers did not differ in gender, but there became a difference depending on their professional experience.

Adedayo(2015) investigated the predicting effects of computer self-efficacy, computer competency, commitment to ethical goodness and community bonding on the Internet self-efficacy of pre-service teachers' in South-West, Nigeria. A field-based approach was adopted to collect quantitative data through the use of a questionnaire from 1285 pre-service teachers that were randomly sampled in four universities in Nigeria. Multiple regression statistical analysis employed showed that the independent variables were good predictors of pre-service teachers' Internet self efficacy. Results showed the need for teachers' training institutions to provide

Information and Communication Technology equipments to empower pre service teachers to meet the dynamics needs of schools.

2.3.1 Trend Analysis

A review of the research studies revealed that there is a medium level positive statistical difference between perceived computer self-efficacy and attitudes toward computer. Studies on computer self-efficacy in general also revealed that males on average have better computer self-efficacy than females. Review of studies on computer self-efficacy reveals that it is an important determinant of Internet anxiety (Dinev, 2002), and a significant relationship between computer anxiety and attitudes towards internet was found (Sam, Othman and Nordin, 2005). Computer self-efficacy has been reported to be the best predictor of computer anxiety (Embi, 2007). Perceived self-efficacy is thought to be a critical factor that influences learners' satisfaction with the Blackboard e-learning system (Liaw, 2008), and, a high computer literacy level is related to computer use (Ocak and Akdemir, 2008). Computer self efficacy plays a role in reducing the strength and significance of the impact of anxiety on perceived ease of use and having a strong and significant relationship with computer anxiety (Saade and Kira, 2009), also, a positive relationship has been reported between attitudes towards e-learning and computer self-efficacy, and a negative relation between computer self-efficacy and computer anxiety (Omidian, 2010). It is finally concluded that perceived usefulness and perceived ease of use is helpful in predicating the success of E-learning adoption (Alenezi, Abdul Karim & Veloo, 2010).

2.4 RESEARCH STUDIES RELATED TO SELF REGULATION

Tillema (1999) investigated the difference in perceptions among teacher educators and prospective teachers about implementation and expected behaviours of self- regulation as a vehicle for learning in teacher education programmes. Results indicated clear support for the concept of self-regulated learning. Prospective teachers were found to have a more positive attitude toward self-regulated learning and higher expectations about their own self-regulative competencies than their teachers, who seemed more concerned with their students' preparation for the profession. They suggested that self-regulation in teacher education programmes requires new ways of interaction between teacher educators and their students.

Pintrich (2000) conducted a study to find correlation between motivational orientation, self-regulated learning and classroom academic performance. Data were collected from 173 seventh graders from 8 science and 7 English classes. A self-report measure of student self-efficacy, intrinsic value, test anxiety, self-regulation and use of learning strategies was administered, and performance data were obtained from work on classroom assignments. They found positive relation between cognitive engagement and performance. Regression analysis revealed that, depending on the outcome measure, self-regulation, self-efficacy and test anxiety emerged as the best predictors of performance. Findings revealed that intrinsic value did not have a direct influence on performance but was strongly related to self-regulation and cognitive strategy use, regardless of prior achievement level.

Lee et al. (2000) examined the relationships between Meta-cognition, self-regulation and students' critical thinking skills and disposition in online Socratic Seminars for ninth grade World Geography and Culture students. The sample for the study was drawn from 9th grade classes in a public high school in south central Texas in the United States. They were randomly assigned to two groups: a three class treatment group and a three class comparison group. Students in both groups received training on critical thinking skills, Internet security, and the technological tools involved in the online Socratic Seminars. The experimental group performed two Meta-cognitive tasks. Both quantitative and qualitative data were collected and analysed. A multivariate analysis of covariance (MANCOVA) showed statistically significant effects of the two meta-cognitive tasks on student's self-regulation, but not on their critical thinking skills and disposition. The structure equation modelling analysis showed that self-regulation had significant relationships with students' critical thinking disposition, but not with students' critical thinking skills for both the experimental and the comparison groups. The structural equation modelling analysis also revealed an insignificant moderating effect of performing the two Meta-cognitive tasks on the relationship between self-regulation and students' critical thinking.

Joo et al. (2000) examined the relationship among gender, self-efficacy for self- regulated learning, academic self-efficacy, computer experiences, internet self- efficacy and academic achievement in web-based courses on 152 high school students. A path analysis revealed that students' self-efficacy for self-regulated learning was positively correlated with academic self-efficacy. However, students' academic achievement and internet self-efficacy were not the significant factors in terms of predicting the performance.

Harner et al. (2000) compared the self-regulation in the distance education context and the traditional context. They employed a forty item instrument designed to measure the effect of video technology on students, distance learning-related self- regulatory behaviours and self-efficacy. They found significant difference in self regulation of distance education learning and traditional learning. They also found that students who had taken online courses previously scored higher on study skills than those who had not.

Peklaj and Pecjak (2002) conducted a study on self-regulated learning in high school students. The result showed that girls have greater knowledge about the role of thinking in self-regulation of learning, use more metacognitive strategies and more intrinsically motivated to express more feelings related to learning.

Graham & Shaw (2003) conducted a study to examine whether background knowledge and note-taking strategies would be positively related to self-regulation. Results indicated that college students were not good at self-regulation, they found no correlation in background knowledge and note taking. They suggested that note taking and background knowledge were generally better predictors of test performance than self-regulation. Results revealed that test performance is more related to note taking and background knowledge than to self-regulation.

Richard (2004) reviewed the distance education and self-regulation literatures to identify learner self-regulation skills predictive of academic success in a blended education context. Five self-regulatory attributes were judged likely to be predictive of academic performance: intrinsic goal orientation, self-efficacy for learning and performance, time and study environment management, help seeking, and Internet self-efficacy. Verbal ability was used as a control measure. Performance was operationalized as final course grades. Data were collected from 94 students in a blended undergraduate marketing course. Regression analysis revealed that verbal ability and self-efficacy related significantly to performance.

Karen (2006) studied the effect of self-regulated strategy development (SRSD). Instruction focused on planning and writing stories and persuasive essays. The addition of a peer support component to SRSD instruction aimed at facilitating maintenance and generalization effects was also examined. SRSD had a positive impact on the writing performance and knowledge of struggling second-grade writers attending urban schools serving a high percentage of low-income families. Moreover, the peer support component augmented SRSD instruction by enhancing specific aspects of students' performance in both the instructed and uninstructed genres.

Keech (2007) investigated the effect of task difficulty and self-regulated practice strategies on motor learning. The task was to move a mouse-operated cursor through pattern arrays that differed in two levels of difficulty. Participants learned either four easy or hard patterns after assignment to one of four groups that ordered practice in blocked, random, self-regulated and yoked-to-self-regulated schedules. Although individual switch strategies for members of the self-regulated groups were quite variable, the impact of self-regulation on motor learning remained similar. Finding revealed that self regulated practices were important variable for motor learning.

Sitzmann (2008) reviewed the current state of research on self-regulated learning and gaps in the field's understanding of how adults regulate their learning of work-related knowledge and skills. Self-regulation theory was used as a conceptual lens for deriving a heuristic framework of 16 fundamental constructs that constitute self- regulated learning. Meta-analytic findings supported theoretical propositions that self regulation constructs were interrelated—30% of the corrected correlations among constructs were .50 or greater. However, there was no significant relationship with learning found in four self-regulatory processes, planning, monitoring, help seeking and emotion control.

Winters & Costich (2008) analyzed empirical and peer-reviewed articles which were focused on examining the relationship between self-regulated learning and academic learning in computer-based learning environments. They concluded that students adapted self-regulated learning strategies in taking online courses. In addition, students demonstrating high achievement or more learning gain tended to use more self-regulated learning strategies than those who exhibited lower achievement and less learning gain.

Yukselturk & Bulut (2009) conducted research to find gender

differences in self- regulated learning in online learning settings. The sample consisted of 145 participants. MLSQ was used as their measure to determine the self-regulated learning components, the levels of motivation beliefs and achievement. Based on the regression results, they found that only test anxiety can statistically significantly predict female students' achievement, while self-efficacy for learning and performance and task value were the statistically significant predictors for male students' achievement. However, they did not find any gender differences in terms of the level of self-regulated learning based on the MANOVA results.

Clarebout et al. (2010) investigated whether embedding support may provide a solution to sub optimal use of support and whether this is related to learners' self-regulation skills and goal orientation. Sixty students were divided in a condition where support was embedded and a condition where support was non-embedded. Results revealed that the embedded group used more and spent more time on the use of support. Quality of use differed for one support device only, with quality being higher in the non-embedded group. An interaction with self-regulation was found. High self-regulators use the support devices less optimally when support is embedded. They found that

Quality of usage and proportional time spent on support influenced learning outcomes.

Bernardo (2011) investigated the efficacy of an intervention program in virtual format intended to train studying and self-regulation strategies to university students. The program had been developed in Moodle format and hosted by the Virtual Campus of the University of Oviedo. The present study had a semi-experimental design, included an experimental group (n=167) and a control one (n=206), and used pre test and post test measures. Study revealed that the students enrolled in the training program, comparing with students in the control group, showed a significant improvement in their declarative knowledge, general and on text use of learning strategies, increased their deep approach to learning, decreased their use of a surface approach and, in what concerns to academic achievement, statistically significant differences have been found in favour of the experimental group.

James (2011) investigated the effect of self-regulated learning strategies (SRLS) on performance in a learner-controlled and a program-controlled computer-based instruction (CBI). The data collected using a self-regulated learning strategies questionnaire. Seventh-grade subjects were divided into high and low levels of SRLS and then randomly assigned to one of two versions of a CBI lesson: one allowing learner control over the sequence and content of the instruction and the other having the learners follow a linear instructional sequence. Results revealed that the performance differences between learners with high SRLS and those with low SRLS were greater under learner control than under program control.

Dangwal (2011) attempted to find out whether school-going children who are exposed to the Hole-in-the-Wall Education Limited (HiWEL) learning station are higher on self regulatory behaviour as compared to school going children who are not exposed to HiWEL learning station. Results indicated that children in the age range 8 to 14 years using HiWEL learning station are self regulated learners. This study is exploratory, the results were very encouraging and point in the direction that HiWEL learning station plays a vital role in enabling children to become self-regulated learners.

Rouis's (2011) conducted research to test the perceived effect of personality traits, self-regulation and trust on students' achievements. Paper and pencil survey was run with undergraduate students from Lulea University of Technology and data from 239 students was used to test the model. Smart PLS software was employed to test the proposed structural equation model. Results indicated an extensive use of Facebook by students with extraverted personalities lead to poor academic performance. He also found that students' cognitive absorption with Facebook is only regulated by their self-control and their personality traits, which determines how much time they spend on Facebook. Results supported that Self-regulation and performance goal orientation characterized the students who are more in control of this social activity.

Johnson (2012) investigated self-regulatory strategies that are integrated into Physics problem solving. It also took Meta-cognitive awareness among the students as a chief component of self-regulatory strategies and multimedia as a component of motivation. The investigation was carried out in S.R.V.S Higher Secondary school, Karaikal on
90 students, 45 students belong to computer Science and 45 students belong to Biology group. The students were divided into control and experimental group based on the mathematical ability and Physics achievement score. The major findings of the study revealed that there exists marked difference between Post-test1 and post-test2 for the

following variables of experimental group in Physics problem solving ability, self regulatory awareness and knowledge of ICT and students attitude towards learning Physics.

Toussi & Ghanizadeh (2012) investigated the relationship between EFL teacher's locus ofcontrol and self regulation. Data were collected from the 63 English teachers through convenience sampling method from different language institutes of Mashhad. The teachers were asked to complete Teacher Self-Regulation Scale as well as the Teacher Locus of Control Scale. The data supported a linkage between self-regulation and locus of control. The results indicated a significant relationship between teachers' self-regulation and internal locus of control. Subsequent data analyses indicated that among the components of self-regulation, 'mastery goal orientation', and 'intrinsic interest' have the highest correlations with teacher locus of control. The findings also illustrated that teacher self-efficacy had no significant impact on the relationship between self-regulation and locus of control.

Huang (2013) examined the self regulation levels in attention and reading comprehension of the two groups. Data were collected from the 126 Grade 7 students in four classes at a junior high school in New Taipei City, Taiwan. Among the four classes, two classes were randomly distributed to the experimental group and the other two classes were randomly distributed to the control group. The experimental group utilized the ASRLM to support their reading of annotated English texts online, whereas the control group is not supported by the ASRLM while reading annotated English texts online. Experimental results showed that sustained attention and reading comprehension of the experimental group are better than those of the control group. Moreover, the web-based reading system with ASRLM support promotes the sustained attention and reading comprehension of female learners more than those of male learners while reading annotated English texts online. Additionally, learners with high-SRL ability in the experimental group have better sustained attention and reading comprehension than those learners with low-SRL ability. Furthermore, the sustained attention and reading comprehension of the experimental group are strongly correlated and the duration of sustained attention strongly predicts their reading comprehension performance.

Lin (2015) investigated the impact of network centrality and self-regulation on student learning in e-learning environment. Results revealed that the student group with high-level centrality and low-level self-regulation more significantly progresses in learning achievement than the other groups. The second finding showed that the group also had the highest number of students asking for help.

Mahlberg (2015) studied the influence of formative self-assessment on community college student's self-regulatory practices. The students were enrolled in two classes one is self-assessment and second is traditional assessment class. Students completed the Motivated Strategies for Learning Questionnaire (MSLQ) as a measure of self- regulation. A significant difference was found in self-reported self-regulation in self- assessment class and traditional assessment classes. Result revealed a significant and positive correlation in behavioral and motivational variables. Further, results indicated a robust effect of instructor on self-regulation.

2.4.1 Trend Analysis

Graham & Shaw (2003); Sitzmann (2008); Rouis (2011) revealed that test performance is more related to note taking and background knowledge than to self- regulation. Johnson (2012); Karen (2006); Keech (2007); Winter & Costich

(2008); Huang (2013) noted that self-regulatory strategies with interactive multimedia effective for enhancing problem solving ability among higher secondary students. Murtagh (2004) suggested that an individual's capacity to self-regulate is limited, and easily depleted. James (2011); Lin (2005) revealed that the performance difference between learners with high SRLS and those with low SRLS were greater under learner control than under program control. Mahlberg (2015) supported robust effect of instructor on self-regulation and a significant increase in retention for students enrolled in self-assessment classes. Lin (2015) indicated that the student group with high-level centrality and low-level of self-regulation more significantly progresses in learning achievement than the other groups.

2.5 RELATED STUDIES RELATED TO TECHNOLOGY INTEGRATION BELIEFS

Harris & Grandgenett (1999) found no significant correlation between teacher's beliefs and use of technology. However, they also cautioned that the findings could be due to a design issue where no distinction was made between teacher's use of technology for teaching and for personal use. In this study, teachers who reported a high level of innovativeness in the use of technology also perceived themselves as more student-centred in their teaching practices.

Becker and Wong (2000) found that teachers who used technology more extensively also reported greater changes in their teaching practices in a constructivist direction. In a constructivist situation, learners undergo a process in which they actively construct knowledge and create product that are personally meaningful. Under such circumstances, the teacher acts as a facilitator to guide students to make sense of information. However, direct connection between a student-centred, constructivist approach to teaching and use of technology in the classroom is often unwarranted without empirical study.

Pierson (2001) studied the relationship among the technology integration practices, individual teachers' levels of teaching expertise, their definition of technology integration, and pedagogical expertise. This finding supported the connection among teachers' personal beliefs about teaching and learning, pedagogical knowledge, and technology integration. Results reported that teachers who effectively integrated technology showed good understandings of unique characteristics of various types of technologies, and were able to draw content, pedagogical and technological knowledge all together.

Cope (2002) conducted a study to highlight the importance of appropriate perceptions to successful integration of learning technologies into classrooms. The transcripts of 31 semi-structured, open-ended interviews with a group of teachers were combined to form a pool of de contextualized statements about learning technologies. The pools of statements were analyzed using a phenomenon graphic research approach. A limited number of qualitatively different perceptions of learning technologies were identified. Some of the perceptions were considered inappropriate with regard to the "how" component and unlikely to lead to successful integration.

Zhao (2003) reviewed the potential of technology for improving language education. The review found that existing literature on the effectiveness of technology uses in language education is very limited in four aspects: a) The number of systematic, well- designed empirical evaluative studies of the effects of technology uses in language learning is very small,

b) the settings of instruction where the studies conducted were limited to higher education and adult learners, c) the language studied was limited to common foreign language and English as a foreign or second language, and d)the experiments were often short-term and about one or two aspects of language learning. However the limited number of available studies shows a pattern of positive effects. They found that technology supported language learning was at least as effective as human teachers.

Hernandez-Ramos (2005) conducted a survey to find the technology use in K-12 schools. The researcher pointed out the broad context of technology integration process and concluded that: as well as personality factors, the technological and contextual factors play crucial roles in technology integration decisions and applications. Hernandez-Ramos pointed out that barriers to technology integration might differ according to different context. Since without having necessary contribution it is difficult to use and infuse technology, technological and computer skills as required. Without faith, it will be hard to be creative, innovative and curious about technology, so beliefs and attitudes toward new technologies and computers would also be a crucial step in the technology integration process.

Angers & Machtmes (2005) investigated the beliefs, context factors and practices of three middle school exemplary teachers that led to a technology-enriched curriculum. Findings suggested that these middle school teachers believe technology was a tool that adds value to lessons and to student's learning and motivation.

Niess (2005) investigated Pre service teacher's pedagogical content knowledge (PCK) development with respect to integrating technology. Four components of PCK were adapted to describe technology enhanced PCK (TPCK). The study examined the TPCK of student teachers in a multi-dimensional science and mathematics teacher preparation program that integrated the teaching and learning with technology throughout the program. Five cases described the difficulties and successes of student teachers teaching with technology in moulding their TPCK.

Levin (2006) investigated and interpreted the evolution of teachers' beliefs regarding learning, teaching and technology and their instructional practices, in the context of integrating technology based information in six 4th-6th grade classrooms. The study used multiple research tools, interviews, questionnaires and observations, focusing on both teachers' beliefs and classroom practices. The findings revealed that following multi-year experiences in technology based classrooms; teachers' educational beliefs had changed quitted substantively, demonstrating multiple views rather than pure beliefs. The study supported teachers' beliefs from a mosaic of complementary visions, even were conflicting one. It also showed that it is easier to change classroom practices than educational beliefs.

Judson (2006) indicated that teachers who readily integrate technology into their instruction are more likely to possess constructivist teaching styles. Evidence showed that there is a parallel between a teacher's student-centred beliefs about instruction and the nature of the teacher's technology-integrated lessons. In this study classroom teachers completed a survey to measure their beliefs about instruction, but they were also directly observed and rated with the Focus on Integrated Technology: Classroom Observation Measurement. Analysis did not reveal a significant relationship between practices and beliefs. Although most teachers identified strongly with constructivist convictions they failed to exhibit these ideas in their practices.

Anderson (2007) investigated factors related to students' technology-related abilities, beliefs, and intentions. Data were collected from 76 pre service teachers who responded to pre-and post-course surveys while taking an introductory educational technology course. Statistically significant changes were found in student's perceived abilities, self-efficacy beliefs, value beliefs, and intentions to use software in their future classrooms. Students' self-efficacy, value beliefs and intentions were moderately correlated with each other. Abilities were correlated with self-efficacy and computer access. These results strongly supported the effectiveness of educational technology coursework in improving not just abilities, but also beliefs and intentions.

Zhao (2007) investigated the perspectives and experiences of social studies teachers following technology integration training. The research indicated that teachers held a variety of views towards technology integration. These views influenced their use of technology in the classroom. It was found that technology integration training increased their use of technology in the classroom and used technology more creatively.

Pan (2008) examined effect of pre-service teacher's behaviour pattern on student teachers' self-efficacy for technology integration through the school year of 2004-

2005. Quantative research was conducted using a paper-and-pencil questionnaire, administered twice in each of the three semesters in the year. One hundred and sixty four students from a U.S. southern state university on the border with Mexico successfully participated on a voluntary basis. Results from t-test and two-way ANOVA analysis suggested that students' self-efficacy for technology integration increased significantly throughout each semester and was affected by students' prior experience with the computer.

Gulbahar (2008) conducted a study to explore to what extent the cause instructional Technology and Material Development," from a non-thesis graduate teacher's preparation programme, contributed to pre-service teachers' perceived computer competencies, attitudes towards computers and technology vision. The participants were under fourteen pre service teachers with a degree from the faculty of Arts & Science. Both quantitative and qualitative measures were used to collect data in order to validate the findings. Participants were asked to fill out computer attitude scale and a computer competency scale both at the beginning and end of the course, as well as an open ended questionnaire at the end of the course. Besides, The results showed that pre-service teachers developed a positive attitude towards using computers in their future classrooms and enhanced their computer competencies.

Muellar et.al (2008) surveyed a random sample of a heterogeneous group of 185 elementary 204 secondary teachers in order to provide a comprehensive summary of teacher's characteristics and variables that best discriminate between teacher who integrated computer and those who do not. Discriminant function analysis indicated seven variables for elementary teachers and six for secondary teachers that discriminated high and low integrators. Variables included positive teaching experiences with computers; teacher's comfort with computer; belief supporting the use of computer as instructional tools; training; motivation; support; and teaching efficacy.

David Hung (2008) examined the relationship between teachers' beliefs about teaching and uses of technology. The study revealed that beliefs in constructivists teaching correlated significantly with both constructivists and traditional uses of technology. However, a belief in traditional teaching is only significantly correlated (negatively) with constructivist use of technology.

Yildirim (2009) investigated the main barriers and possible enablers for integrating information and communication technology (ICTs) in Turkey's pre service teacher's education programme. The data were collected by means of questionnaires of 53 deans in schools of teacher education (STE) 111 teacher educators and 1330 prospective teachers and additionally from interviews of 6 teacher's educators and six prospective teachers. The findings indicated that the majority of the stake holders believed that lack of in-service training, lack of appropriate software and materials and lack of hardware were the main barriers for integrating ICTs in pre-service teacher's education programmes.

Lowther (2009) examined the direct and indirect effects of teacher's individual characteristics and perceptions of environmental factors that influence their technology integration in the classroom. A research-based path model was developed to explain causal relationships between these factor and was tested based on data gathered from 1382 Tennessee public school teachers. The results provided significant evidence that the developed model is useful in explaining factors affecting technology integration and the relationships between the factors.

Palak and Walls (2009) conducted a mixed study to investigate whether teachers who frequently integrate technology and work at technology-rich schools shift their beliefs and practices toward a student-centred paradigm. The results showed that their practices did not change; neither student-centred nor teacher-centred beliefs are powerful predictors of practices. However, teacher's attitudes toward technology significantly predict teacher and student technology use, as well as the use of a variety of instructional strategies.

Sang et al. (2010) indicated that pre-service teachers with highly constructivist teaching beliefs have stronger intentions to integrate technology into their future teaching practices. Furthermore, more confident pre-service teacher was more capable of and interested in using computers in real classrooms. Thus, although teachers' attitudes towards ICT use were found to be the strongest predictor of technology integration, the impact of their beliefs and confidence in using ICT should not be disregarded either.

Almekhalfi & Almeqdadi (2010) investigated technology integration at UAE Model schools using a mixed method of data collection consisting of focus group interviews

and a questionnaire. A sample consisted of 40 female and 60 male teachers from two schools in Abu Dhabi. Study showed that teachers at both schools are integrating technology in their classes' activities. They use a variety of technologies to promote students' learning. However, methods of integration by male teachers differed in some cases compared to their female colleagues.

Kevin (2011) studied correlation between teacher self-efficacy and technology adoption within an urban K-12 school district. A sample of K-12 faculty members completed a 38-item Likert-type survey designed to measure self-efficacy as it relates to the integration of technology within the classroom. Quantitative data were analyzed using a Pearson product-moment correlation to identify relationships between self- efficacy and technology adoption. The findings revealed a positive correlation between teacher self-efficacy and the integration of technology.

Salehi (2012) examined the high school English teacher's perceptions of the factors discouraging teachers to use ICT in the classroom. A sample of 30 high school English teachers was selected from the five main educational districts in the city of Iran, to respond to a validated questionnaire. Stratified random sampling was used to select equal number of respondents from each educational district. The analysis of the data revealed that insufficient technical supports at schools and little access to internet and ICT prevent teachers to use ICT in the class room. Moreover, shortage of class time was another important discouraging factor for the teachers to integrate ICT into the curriculum.

Mueller (2012) studied factors that impact planning to use computer technologies in the class rooms. He conducted a survey of sample of 185 elementary and 204 secondary teachers was asked to respond to open-ended survey questions in order to understand why integration of computer-based technologies does or does not fit with their teaching philosophy, what, and what characteristics define excellent teachers who integrate technology. Qualitative analysis of open-ended questions integrated that, overall, educators are supportive of computer integration describing the potential of technology using constructivists language, such as "authentic tasks" and "self regulated learning".

Lee (2014) identified how pre-service teachers, self efficacy beliefs for technology integration (SETI) can be improved during the course work intervention, and which of

the course factors has the highest impact on the SETI. This research also attempted to explore a more inclusive path of the direct and indirect influences between SETI and other non-course variables. A total of 136 under graduate's students at a teacher education university in Korea participated in the study. Data analysis illustrated significant increase of prospective teachers' SETI after their completion of education technology course resulting mostly from lesson planning practice.

Darci (2014) conducted survey to identify the attitudes and beliefs of prospective teachers towards technology use in education. He also tried to identify the perceived skills students possess at teacher preparation institution from one mid western state. Four hundred seventy six prospective teacher (N=476) responded to the survey. Technology disposition Scale was used for Teacher Education Students' TDS –T. The instrument has two sub scales technology pre-disposition and technology competence. Within the sub scale of technology pre-disposition, four factors were examined: beliefs in long term value in technology, technology self-concept consisting of self confident and self controllability, technology attitude towards usages and beliefs in short term value of technology. A statically significant correlation was found between technology owner ship and technology disposition.

2.5.1 Trend Analysis:

Harris & Grandgenett (1999); Judson (2006) found no significant correlation between teachers beliefs, practices and use of technology. Kevin (2011); Hung (2008); Zhao (2003); Pan (2008); Lee (2014) found a positive correlation between teachers' self efficacy beliefs and technology integration. Yildirim (2009) found that the majority of the stake holders belief that lack of in-service training, lack of appropriate software and materials, and lack of hardware are the main barriers for integrating ICTs in pre- service teachers education programs. Gulbahar (2008) showed that pre-service teachers deployed a positive attitude towards using computers in their future classrooms and enhanced their computer competencies. Anderson (2007) strongly supported the effectiveness of educational technology course work in improving not just abilities, but also beliefs and intentions. Niess (2005) investigated the pre-service teacher's pedagogical content knowledge (PCK) development with respect to integrating technology. Levin (2006) analyzed interpreted evaluation of teachers, belief regarding learning, teaching and technology and their instructional practices, in the context of integrating technology- based information – rich tasks in six fourth- sixth grade classroom. It also found that it is easier to change classroom practices than educational beliefs. Salehi (2012) and Darci(2014) revelaed that insufficient technical support at schools and little access to internet and ICT prevent teachers to use ICT in the classroom. Moreover, shortage of class time was another important discoursing factor for the teachers to integrate ICT into the curriculum. Sang et. Al (2010) focused on the impact of Chinese Student Teachers, gender, constructivist teaching beliefs, teaching self-efficacy, computer self-efficacy, and computer attitudes on their prospective ICT use. The findings confirmed the result of the study by Palak and Walls (2009) that the strongest predictor of future ICT uses were teachers, attitude towards it. Previous studies indicated that ICT integration is a complex phenomenon (e.g.; Mackey and Mills, 2002; Ng, Miao & Lee, 2010) and technology or computer use among teachers is a complicated process (Chen, 2010; Van Braak, Tondeur and Valcke, 2004). Within years of implementing various technology initiatives in Malysian Education Systems, Ismail, Zakaria and Aziz (2007) reported that teachers' level of technology integration was still low. There are numerous studies in Malaysian context on in-service teachers' technology integration in teaching and learning (: Ismail, et al. 2007; Mahmud, et al. 2007; Mohd Salleh, Mohd Nordin & Mohd Jelas, 2008)

2.6 RESEARCH STUDIES RELATED TO COURSE OUTCOMES

Arbaugh (2000) tried to examine the effect of technological, pedagogical, and students' characteristics in internet-based online courses. Ninety-seven MBA students participated in this study. He found that older and female students reported higher level of perceived learning than younger or male students in online learning settings based on the multiple regression analysis. In his another research in 2004, he found that the degrees of students' perceived learning wa not changed by their prior experience in taking online courses.

Abbott and Faris (2000) examined pre-service teachers' attitude toward the use of computer before and after a semester-long technology literacy course. The results showed that positive attitude toward computers increased after the course because of the instructional approaches, meaningful assignment requiring technology, and supportive faculty. Thus, the authors claimed that teacher education programs should

teach pre-service teachers not only how to use hardware and software, but also how to incorporate computers into their teaching strategies and activities. He noted that small groups and collaborative learning are the most appropriate when introducing new hardware and software because more advanced and experienced teachers can assist those who need more technology learning support.

Arbaugh (2001) examined the relationship among the instructor immediacy behaviour, students' satisfaction, and learning. He defined immediacy behaviour as a nonverbal or verbal communication behaviour which can reduce social and psychological distance between the instructor and the students, such as providing and inviting feedback, using humor, eye contact etc. He found that both instructors' immediacy variables and students' attitudes toward the course software were positively associated with course satisfaction.

Thurmond et al. (2002) examined the relationship between students' satisfaction and the online learning environment by controlling students' gender and the number of prior online courses had taken. They collected responses from 120 students and analyzed the data through correlations and hierarchical regression analysis. The results indicated that students' satisfaction was affected by the online learning environmental factors. However, gender and the number of prior online course taken failed to predict student' satisfaction.

Wang and Newlin (2002) investigated the relationship between technology self- efficacy and students' performance in online courses. They found that students with a higher level of technology self-efficacy tend to have higher final exam grades. However, even though a higher level of technology self-efficacy was related to the exam grades, it failed to predict the final grade at the end of the semester.

Marks et al. (2005) examined the relationship among gender, prior student experience with online courses, student perceived learning and satisfaction. They proposed a model in which students' gender, and prior experience with online courses were the antecedent variables, whereas perceived learning was the mediator, and satisfaction was the outcome variable. Furthermore, they also found that students could not distinguish the difference between perceived learning and satisfaction.

Lim et al. (2006) examined the relationships between course outcomes and learner characteristics in an online learning setting. They used course satisfaction, learning gains, and learning application as the operational variables for course outcomes, while gender, age, distance learning experience, online learning preference over classroom, and work status were used as the operational variables for learner characteristics. One hundred and twenty five students, including 39 males and 86 females, from a program evaluation online course participated in this study. As for the correlation analysis, they found that learning motivation was moderately correlated with course satisfaction, and the regression analysis results indicated that learning motivation can predict student's learning gain.

Puzziferro (2008) conducted study to examine performance as a function of grade and course satisfaction in online undergraduate level course, specifically students' self-efficacy for online technology and self-regulated learning strategies. This research included a sample (N=815) of community college student enrolled in liberal art online courses during a single semester. The results of this study showed that online technologies self-efficacy scores were not correlated with student performance. In addition, rehearsal, elaboration, meta-cognitive self-regulation, and time and study environment were significantly positively correlated with levels of satisfaction.

Paechter (2010) tried to link the relationship among students' expectations of online courses, experience in taking online courses, perceived learning achievement, and course satisfaction. Two hundred one hundred and ninety-six students with 62% females and 37.4% male participated in this research. Multivariate multiple regression analysis results indicated that gender, age, or number of online courses taken could not statistically significantly predict student's performance in online courses. Also, students expectations can positively predict student's achievement, while student's motivation and previous online learning experiences can positively predict both students' achievement and course satisfaction.

Keshavarz (2011) studied a methodology for providing quantitative measurement of a course's learning outcomes. The methodology uses a linkage matrix that associates each course learning outcome to one or more course assessment tool. The approach adopted provide a numeric score between 0 and 1 for each learning outcome with respect to each assessment tool and a combined score be calculated for each learning outcome from the tools associated with that outcome. The proposed methodology also provides insight into the consistency of the various assessment tools used to measure the achievement of a particular course learning outcome.

Yukselturk (2013) investigated online learner profiles in regard to entry, characteristics, participation behaviours and achievement of course outcomes. The data were collected through five online questionnaires included 10 variable (gender, age, work status, self-efficacy, online readiness, self-regulation, participation in discussion list, participation in chat session, satisfaction and achievement) and 186 participants. A two-step cluster analysis, chi-square analysis and multivariate analysis were used to analyze the collected data. The results indicated that online learner fell into three significantly different clusters and within each cluster, learners had a close combination of employment characteristics, gender type, age level, perception of self-efficacy for online technologies and participation behaviour level.

Wang et al. (2013) examined the relationship among student's characteristics, self- regulated learning, technology self-efficacy and course outcomes in online learning settings.

Two hundred and fifty-six students participated in this study. All participants completed an online survey that included demographic information, the modified motivation strategies learning questionnaire, the online technology self-efficacy scale, the course satisfaction questionnaire, and the final grades. The researchers used structural equation modelling to examine relationships among student characteristics, self-regulated learning, technology self-efficacy, and course outcomes. Based on the results from the final model, student with previous online learning experiences tended to have more effective learning strategies when taking online courses and hence, had higher level of motivation in their online course. In addition, when students had higher levels of motivation in their online courses, their levels of technology, self- efficacy and course satisfaction increased.

2.6.1 Trend Analysis

Arbaugh (2001) & Aechter (2010) found that both the instructors' and students' attitudes toward the course software were positively associated with course satisfaction. Wang (2013); Yukselturk (2013); Wang and Newlin (2002) also found students with higher levels of technology self-efficacy and course satisfaction also earned better final grades. Lim et al. (2006) examined the relationships between course outcomes and learner characteristics in an online learning setting. He found that learning motivation was moderately correlated with course satisfaction, and the regression analysis results indicated that learning motivation can predict students' learning gain. Puzziferro (2008) found positive correlation between rehearsal, elaboration, meta-cognitive self-regulation, and time and study environment and course satisfaction.

CHAPTER-III
EMERGENCE OF THE PROBLEM

3.1 RATIONALE OF THE STUDY

With the convergence of technologies, it has become imperative to take a comprehensive look at all possible information and communication technologies for improving school education in the country. The comprehensive choice of ICT for holistic development of education can be built only on a sound policy. The initiative of ICT Policy in School Education is inspired by the tremendous potential of ICT for enhancing outreach and improving quality of education. This policy endeavours to provide guidelines to assist the States in optimizing the use of ICT in school education within a national policy framework. The National Policy on Education 1986, as modified in 1992, stressed the need to employ educational technology to improve the quality of education. The policy statement led to two major centrally sponsored schemes, namely, Educational Technology (ET) and

Computer Literacy and Studies in Schools (CLASS) paving the way for a more comprehensive centrally sponsored scheme – Information and Communication Technology @ Schools in 2004. Educational technology also found a significant place in another scheme on upgradation of science education.

The significant role ICT can play in school education has also been highlighted in the National Curriculum Framework 2005 (NCF). Use of ICT for quality improvement also figures in Government of India's flagship programme on education, Sarva Shiksha Abhiyan (SSA). Again, ICT has figured comprehensively in the norm of schooling recommended by the Central Advisory Board of Education (CABE), in its report on Universal Secondary Education, in 2005. Introducing ICT as a tool to support the education sector has initiated substantial discussions since the late 1990s. A decade ago the emphasis was on Technical and Vocational Education and Training and training teachers. During the last few years an increasing number of international development agencies have embraced the potential of ICT to support the education sector. UNESCO has played a major role in spearheading the Education for All initiative to harness the potential of ICT. The Information and Communication Technology (ICT) curriculum provides a broad perspective on the nature of

technology, how to use and apply a variety of technologies, and the impact of ICT on self and society. During the last two decades higher education institutions have invested heavily in information and communication technologies (ICT). ICT has had a major impact in the university context, in organisation and in teaching and learning methods. One puzzling question is the effective impact of these technologies on student achievement and on the returns of education. Many academic researchers have tried to answer this question at the theoretical and empirical levels. They have faced two main difficulties. On one hand, student performance is hard to observe and there is still confusion about its definition. On the other hand, ICT is evolving technologies and their effects are difficult to isolate from their environment. There is no standard definition for student performance. The standard approach focuses on achievement and curricula, how students understand the courses and obtain their degrees or their marks. However, a more extensive definition deals with competencies, skills and attitudes learned through the education experience. The narrow definition allows the observation of the outcomes of any change in higher education, while the more extensive definition needs a more complex strategy of observation and a focus on the labour market.

According to Wilkins (2008) the relationship between the use of ICT and student performance in higher education is not clear, and there are contradictory results in the literature. Earlier economic research has failed to provide a clear consensus concerning the effect on students' achievement. Technology is about the ways things are done; the processes, tools and techniques that alter human activity. ICT is about the new ways in which people can communicate, inquire, make decisions and solve problems. Enhancing and upgrading the quality of education and instruction is a vital concern, predominantly at the time of the spreading out and development of education.

ICTs can improve the quality of education in a number of ways: By augmenting student enthusiasm and commitment, by making possible the acquirement of fundamental skills and by improving teacher training. ICTs are also tools which enable and bring about transformation which, when used properly, can encourage the shift to an environment which is learner-centered. ICTs which can be in the form of videos, television and also computer multimedia software, that merge sound, transcripts and multi coloured moving imagery, can be made use of so as to make available stimulating, thought provoking and reliable content that will keep the student interested in the learning process. The radio on the other hand through its interactive programs utilizes songs, sound effects, adaptations, satirical comedies and supplementary collections of performances so as to induce the students to listen and get drawn in to the training that is being provided. The use of online pedagogy within universities and management institutes is increasing.

According to Thatcher et al. (2007) the introduction of the Wi-Fi system too has led to the growth of hi-tech education system, where accessibility and accountability of subject matter is made readily available to the students. The students can now study and comprehend the related information at their own convenient time. The application of ICTs as a tool for effective enhancement of learning, teaching and education management covers the entire spectrum of education from early childhood development, primary, secondary, tertiary, basic education and further education and training. Integrating ICT in teaching and learning is high on the educational reform agenda.

Often ICT is seen as an indispensable tool to fully participate in the knowledge society. ICTs need to be seen as "an essential aspect of teaching's cultural tool kit in the twenty-first century, affording new and transformative models of development that extend the nature and reach of teacher learning wherever it takes place" (Leach, 2005). For developing countries like India, ICT can moreover be seen as a way to merge into a globalizing world. It is assumed that ICT brings revolutionary change in teaching methodologies. The innovation lies not per se in the introduction and use of ICT, but in its role as a contributor towards a student centred form of teaching and learning. So it is very essential to the study the effect of information and communication technology skills.

Teachers are currently being asked to become computer literate and to integrate emerging computer technology into their teaching. Because computers are a relatively new phenomenon in education, it is important for educators to understand what level of impact teachers' degrees of computer self-efficacy have on their teaching. computer self-efficacy does have a significant impact on the implementation of computers into classroom teaching, then instruments that can measure computer self-efficacy could aid schools in the development of technology implementation plans that specifically address the needs and abilities of their teachers. The emergence and success of new technology sectors in both new and established educational settings is inextricably linked with individuals able to recognize new opportunities and lead their exploitation. New technology use is advanced by those with self-efficacy, with confidence in their abilities to perform the learning tasks. Computer self-efficacy (CSE) was derived from the social–psychological concept of self-efficacy which postulates that an individuals' perception of his/her abilities affects his/her actual performance (Bandura, 1994). As applied to the field of computer usage, CSE is believed to influence an individual affect, persistence and motivation (Deng, Doll, Truong, 2004) to use that device. CES has been found to influence an individual's willingness to learn and use a computer (Wilfong, 2006), on computer attitudes and utilization (Al-Khaldi & Al-Jabri, 1998). Parayitam et al. (2010) assumes that computer anxiety is a kind of emotional and cognitive reaction that occurs while the individual is working and interacting with computer and it happens as a consequence of the lack of awareness and the individual's attitude towards the computer as a threatening object. Some studies focus self-efficacy and competence on computer anxiety and computer use (Shih, 2006). However, increasing CSE can lower computer anxiety thus improving performance and willingness to learn (Konerding, 1998). Computer use and Computer self-efficacy should be directly related since we are more likely to attempt and persist in behaviors that we feel capable of performing. Confidence or autonomy competence in self-efficacy is considered as one important factor that enhances the flow of intrinsic motivation because learners are given a sense of control over choices they may take in learning (Ryan & Deci, 2000). Quinn (2005) argues that flow is the merging of action and awareness and the other dimensions form the antecedents and consequences of the engagement experience.

In an attempt to understand why technology is differently (or not at all) integrated into teaching among teachers who are equipped with relevant knowledge, two sets of barriers are often discussed (Ertmer, 1999, 2005; Hew & Brush, 2007): (a) first-order barriers concern factors such as environmental readiness (e.g., computers, the Internet access) and teacher knowledge (e.g., TPACK); (b) second-order barriers include factors such as teachers' beliefs

(Ertmer, 1999, 2005; Hew & Brush, 2007). Second-order barriers, defined as the intrinsic factors that hinder technology integration, can interfere with teachers' technology integration even when first-order barriers are overcome (Ertmer, 1999). It has been well documented that technology availability creates the possibility of effective technology integration (Norris, Sullivan, & Poirot, 2003) but knowledge pertinent to pedagogy and content are required to realize the full potential of teaching technologies to improve learning and instruction (Mishra & Koehler, 2006; Shulman, 1987). Nonetheless, the acquisition of technology and knowledge does not always lead to effective technology integration (Polly, Mims, Shepherd, & Inan, 2010). Teachers' persistent beliefs about current practices are recognized as second-order barriers that delay or inhibit technology integration (Ertmer, 2005). Even when technology and technical knowledge are in place (i.e., when first order barriers are overcome), effective technology integration requires teachers' beliefs in "new ways of both seeing and doing things" (Ertmer, 2005). Teachers' beliefs predict, reflect, and determine their actual teaching practice (Kagan, 1992; Pajares, 1992).

Self-regulation is critical for enabling a child to engage in those social experiences that enable him to learn the cognitive and emotion-regulating skills that underpin self-control. A child who has difficulty engaging in these critical social experiences because of the drain on his nervous system can indeed be helped; but only if his or her needs are first understood. Over the past decade there's been an explosion of research on self-regulation in regards to a broad range of mental and physical problems. Each is thought to have unique biological antecedents and/or environmental contingencies, and to follow a different developmental pathway. Even within each disorder there is thought to be enormous variability in the pathways. But each is thought to involve a problem in self regulation, starting early in the child's life. Self-regulation refers to activities in which individuals engage while trying to achieve specific goals. Self-regulatory activities become particularly important when obstacles arise in the course of the pursuit of goals and additional investment of effort is required. Self-regulatory activities are directed at performances in very diverse areas (Boekaerts, Pintrich & Zeidner, 2000), but the focus of this paper is on self-regulatory activities in learning processes. Cognitive psychology defines learning as the acquisition of knowledge, but a broader, perhaps more appropriate definition would hold that learning comprises all activities that increase an individual's knowledge and understanding of the world and that help him to develop skills which he uses to interact meaningfully and successfully with his environment. Self-regulation in learning and instruction has attracted a considerable amount of interest in recent years. At the same time, computers have come to play an important role in today's learning environments. With the advent of the new Information and Communication Technology (ICT), computer programs have become more complex and it can be argued that the high degree of complexity at least requires and possibly affords a higher degree of self- regulation.

The fast growth of ICT, particularly information technology and easy access to information through the Internet and email, is now an undeniable fact of contemporary life and one that is inextricably linked with modern education. As students and teachers begin to use ICT in classrooms, its use has the potential to lead to changes in the role of the teacher and the school. The teacher's role, as described by Scheffler and Logan (1999), should be to work in collaboration with students as knowledge is applied to authentic situations. Teaching no longer centres on the transfer of content from teacher to student. Instead, learning comes from student inquiry, critical thinking and problem solving based on information accessed from a variety of sources. As Godfrey (2001) states, "to become confident, critical and creative users of ICT, teachers must have access to professional development programs that enable them to have multiple skills, both, in the use of technology and in task design". Therefore teachers need, not only the ICT skills, but also the models of best practice and knowledge to support learning. They need to understand the rationale for integrating ICT into learning environments and interpreting curriculum documents to make decisions about designing, delivering, managing and evaluating instruction. The process of integrating technology into classroom work has emerged as a significant focus of study in educational research. Interest in this trend has been motivated by the growing number of technology projects implemented in schools. Investigative findings concur in emphasizing the complexity of the phenomenon. For researchers such as Hernandez-Ramos (2005) technology integration should be defined not simply as a question of access but rather as a tool both for improving educators' professional productivity and promoting student learning. Within this analytical framework, studies such as Lawless and Pellegrino (2007) asserted that even though in-service training is officially recognized as a fundamental vehicle for teachers to develop more effective instruction using new technologies in teaching and learning processes, technology has not been sufficiently incorporated into school work and has yet to be properly articulated with other classroom teaching activities. In other words, although in-service training programmes have contributed to the growing understanding of the potential of technology for the construction of learning, technology integration will only be achieved to the extent educators can link the tool in a natural and logical manner to the normal flow of the school curriculum, a state of affairs that has yet to be fully achieved in educational institutions (Cuban 2001; Mills & Tincher 2003).

According to an Essay, UK (2013) there is growing interest in the integration of technology into the classroom. A large number of initiatives have been launched to develop prospective teacher training processes that will strengthen this integration. One of the reasons for this situation is rooted in the initial training of teachers where the use of technology tends to be a mere adjunct to the syllabus for activities such as information searches. Used in this manner, technology will not be integrated pedagogically and will therefore not serve as a source of experiences that can be articulated with the teachers' professional activities. As a result, teacher training scenarios in this area are weak and do not target the development of a critical and purposeful analysis of the possible relationships between technology and school. A central requirement for teacher training processes is to turn out skilled educators who can perform their labours in dynamic and heterogeneous situations and have the necessary competencies for integrating their knowledge in support of decisions related to the challenges of their professional activity. As it has been highlighted above, there is mismatch between present day scenario and the actual understanding of the subjects by the students. This is because of existing teaching methodology and instructional which lacks innovation. Thus the investigator has chosen the following problem in the light of the studies discussed above.

3.2 STATEMENT OF THE PROBLEM

EFFECT OF INFORMATION AND COMMUNICATION TECHNOLOGY SKILLS DEVELOPMENT PROGRAM ON COMPUTER SELF EFFICACY, SELF REGULATION, TECHNOLOGY INTEGRATION BELIEFS AND COURSE OUTCOMES OF PROSPECTIVE TEACHERS

3.3 OBJECTIVES

The main objectives of the study were:

1. To develop and validate Information and Communication Technology (ICT) skills development program for prospective teachers.
2. To compare the effect of Information and Communication Technology (ICT) skills development program and traditional instruction on computer self efficacy of prospective teachers.
3. To compare the effect of Information and Communication Technology (ICT) skills development program and traditional instruction on self regulation of prospective teachers.
4. To compare the effect of Information and Communication Technology (ICT) skills development program and traditional instruction on technology integration beliefs of prospective teachers.
5. To compare the effect of Information and Communication Technology (ICT) skills development program and traditional instruction on course outcomes with respect to Computer achievement and

satisfaction of prospective teachers.

3.4 HYPOTHESES

H_1 There is no significant difference in the mean gain scores on computer self efficacy of prospective teachers exposed to different instructional treatment.

Further hypothesis were formulated to analyse mean gain scores on computer self efficacy with respect to the three domains.

The two instructional treatments yield equal mean

difference scores on: $H_{1.01}$ Beginning skills

$H_{1.02}$ File and Software skills $H_{1.03}$ Advancing Skills

H_2 There is no significant difference in the mean gain scores on self regulation of prospective teachers exposed to different instructional treatment.

Further hypothesis were formulated to analyse mean gain scores on self regulation with respect to the seven domains.

The two instructional treatments yield equal mean difference scores on:

H₃ There is no significant difference in the mean gain scores on technology integration beliefs of prospective teachers exposed to different instructional treatments.

H₄ There is no significant difference in the mean gain scores on course outcomes of prospective teachers exposed to different instructional treatments with respect to computer achievement.

H₅ There is no significant difference in the mean scores on course outcomes of prospective teachers exposed to different instructional treatments with respect to course satisfaction.

3.5 DELIMITATIONS OF THE STUDY

1. The present study was conducted on B.Ed students of Indo Global College of Education, Abhipur, Distt. Mohali and International Divine College of Education, Ratwara Sahib, Mullanpur, Distt. Mohali, affiliated to Punjabi University, Patiala.
2. The study was limited to only computer application paper of B.Ed curriculum of Punjabi University, Patiala.
3. The Instructional treatment was limited to 35 sessions of forty minutes duration.

4. The course outcomes were limited to two aspects computer achievement and course satisfaction with instructional program.

CHAPTER – IV
DEVELOPMENT AND DESCRIPTION OF THE TOOLS

The preceding chapters dealt with the theoretical basis of the problem, review of related studies and significance of the study along with objective and hypotheses of the study. The present chapter is devoted to the development and description of the tools required for collection of the data. The following tools have been used for the purpose.

4.1 INFORMATION AND COMMUNICATION TECHNOLOGY SKILLS DEVELOPMENT INSTRUCTIONAL PROGRAM (Developed and validated by the investigator)

4.2 COMPUTER SELF EFFICACY SCALE (CSE) (Embi, 2007)

4.3 SELF REGULATION QUESTIONNAIRE (Brown, Miller & Lawendowski, 1999)

4.4 TECHNOLOGY INTEGRATION BELIEFS SCALE. (Developed and validated by the investigator)

4.4 COMPUTER ACHIEVEMENT TEST (Developed and validated by the investigator)

4.5 COURSE SATISFACTION QUESTIONNAIRE (CSQ) (Frey, Yankelov and Faul, 2003)

4.1 Development of Information and Communication Technology Skills Development Instructional Program

To conduct the experimental study, a computer based skills development program was developed and validated by the investigator in relevance to the content matter being taught. To prepare an instructional program that can supplement prospective teachers classroom teaching, a thorough knowledge of the course content and competence to convert that course into courseware is must. The instructional program is generally designed to serve particular objectives and a particular class or groups. Hence it is necessary to determine and consider the needs and capabilities of learners for whom the instructions are being planned.

The computer based information and communication technology skills development instructional program was prepared in three stages:

- Planning the information and communication technology skills development instructional program
- Designing the information and communication technology skills development instructional program
- Validating the information and communication technology skills development instructional program

4.1.1 PLANNING THE INFORMATION AND COMMUNICATION TECHNOLOGY SKILLS DEVELOPMENT INSTRUCTIONAL PROGRAM

Planning an instructional program is a crucial step on which depends the entire process of learning. Hence sufficient thought and time was devoted to this aspect. Experts and teachers were consulted at each step. Steps of developing instructional design were strictly adhered to. Following steps were followed for planning the information and communication technology skills development instructional program:

I. Selection of content
II. Specifying the terminal performance objectives
III. Deciding strategy for program administration
IV. Incorporating computers on ICT

4.1.2 SELECTION OF CONTENT

- For the content, paper of computer application in syllabus of B.Ed students of Punjabi University Patiala was selected.
- It is totally Practical paper of 50 marks.
- Subject experts (Mr. Bhupinder Singh, HOD, Department of Computer Science Engineering, Abhipur; Dr Vidhi Bhalla, Assistant Professor, M.M college of Education, Mullana; Dr Rohit Bhandari, Assistant Professor, Dev Samaj College of Education, Chandigarh; Dr. Harneet Billing, Assistant Professor, Indo Global College of Education, Abhipur; Maneet Sharma, Assistant Professor, Pine Groove College of Education, Bassi Pathana; Dr. Prerna Joshi, PGT (English) Bhavan Vidyalaya School, Panchkula; Dr.

Harpreet Kaur, Principal, I.D College of Education, Ratwara Sahib; Dr Vandana Sharma, Assistant Professor, Indo Global College of Education, Abhipur; Mrs. Seema Malik, Assistant Professor, S.I.E.R, Mohali) were refereed for their views about the topic taken and distribution of content matter.

The Sequential arrangement of subject matter into various chapters has been given as below:

Table 4.1: Chapter Wise Sequential Arrangement of Selected Content Chapter 1: Computer Components & Its working

- Introduction to computers
- Basic operations of Computer system
- Generation of computers
- Desktop properties
- Application of computers

Chapter 2: Introduction to Internet

- Features of the Internet
- World Wide Web
- Web browsers and Search Engines
- E-Mail
- Downloading Files from Web Pages

Chapter 3: Use of Skype
- Features of Skype
- Video calling with Skype
- Chat with Skype
- Video conferencing

Chapter 4: Introduction to Word
- Features of MS word
- Opening /Creating /Saving /Closing word Document
- Insert Pictures
- Find and Replace
- Page setup

Chapter 5: Editing and Formatting text in MS word

- Features of formatting bar
- Select, Moving, Copying and deleting Text
- Using Undo and Redo
- Using auto correct
- Using thesaurus
- Applying font formats
- Text Alignment
- Changing indents and spacing
- Spell checking and Grammar

Chapter 6: Creating and Formatting Tables in MS word

- Creating a Table
- Changing Format of a Table
- Editing text in table
- Applying Border and Shading

Chapter 7: Printing

- Using Print Preview
- How to Print Documents
- Page Setup
- Adjusting Margins
- Types of Printers

Chapter 8: Introduction to PowerPoint

- Features of MS PowerPoint
- Component of A slide Presentation
- Creating new Presentation
- Opening, Saving and Closing a Presentation

Chapter 9: Adding and Formatting Presentation in MS PowerPoint

- Add Text on a Slide
- Change Text Formats
- Using the Paint Format
- Adding Bullets
- Text Alignment

Chapter 10: Slide Transitions & Animation
- Adding a slide
- Changing Slide Layout
- Adding Picture
- Adding Header and footers
- Arrange Slide Show
- Inserting video clip
- Adding Animation Effects
- Add a Sound Clip
- Add a Table
- Add a Chart
- Add Smart Art

4.1.3 SPECIFYING THE TERMINAL PERFORMANCE AND OBJECTIVES The terminal performance and objectives specify the expected final performance. Specification of terminal performance is therefore, the highest level of intellectual development in the package. The terminal performance was based on the students achievement that were expected to demonstrate after the process of instruction was over.

Statement of Instructional objectives

At the end of the instructional program students will be able to:
1. Recall the generations of computer

2.	Define computer
3.	Name components of computer
4.	Different storage devices
5.	Define internet
6.	Recognise the input devices
7.	Name different search engines
8.	Define output device
9.	Recognise the output devices from given list
10.	State effect of viruses
11.	State the steps to open the word document
12.	Create document
13.	Name the components of file menu

14.	Name tools available on formatting bar
15.	Name different font styles
16.	Recognise font styles
17.	Name types of printer
18.	Tell components of PowerPoint
19.	List function of Skype
20.	State function of MS word
21.	State function of MS PowerPoint
22.	Match shortcut key with their function
23.	List different function of MS PowerPoint
24.	Choose the tool from formatting tool bar
25.	Write procedure to insert a column in table
26.	Write procedure to insert row in table
27.	Name different page layout
28.	Recall the files formats
29.	Manage the file structure of a computer
30.	Classify various input and output devices
31.	Classify storage devices
32.	Identify properties of desktop
33.	Formulate email id
34.	Summarize how to save document in MS word
35.	Identify browsers
36.	Organize email folders
37.	Illustrate moving the text
38.	Compare undo and Redo
39.	Match font formats
40.	Recognise shortcut key to spell check
41.	Identify border shading
42.	Identify page layouts
43.	Name the save document
44.	Indicate text format

45. Identify different bar
46. Compare the font size
47. Interpret procedure of chat in Skype
48. Interpret the procedure of downloading

49.	Compose the e mail
50.	Classify the toolbars
51.	Judge the line spacing and indent
52.	Identify and use icons
53.	Adjust margin in word document
54.	Demonstrate the page setup
55.	Use Skype
56.	Show how to chat with Skype
57.	Construct the table
58.	Find missing word from file
59.	Replace word in MS word file
60.	Construct PowerPoint slide
61.	Use thesaurus
62.	Tell how to change slide layout
63.	Perform changing text formats
64.	Perform print preview
65.	Identify shortcut key or their function
66.	Identify the function key
67.	Arrange data in ascending and descending order
68.	Write text messages in Skype
69.	Download and save file on a hard disk

Deciding strategy for the package administration

A strategy based on the utilization of information communication and technology skills development instructional program through learning condition was chosen. This was done since the investigator, who himself taught in the B.Ed college, felt that these topics could be used best through computer program.

4.1.4 DESIGNING OF ICT SKILLS DEVELOPMENT INSTRUCTIONAL PROGRAM

Each lesson of ICT skills development program comprised of following key elements:

Name of the topic: The entire subject matter was divided into 10 chapters. These chapters were further into various sub chapters which have been described earlier.

Instructional Objectives: The instructional objectives were formulated lesson wise for the prospective teachers to specify their terminal performance and their learning outcome. It was done to determine the previous knowledge of the students on the concerned topic before introducing them to new topic.

Demonstration: Various parameter of the content demonstrated thoroughly by the investigator with the help of digital classroom fully equipped with latest equipment. Once students were acquaint with the ICT skills. It was presented them to analyze.

Self practice of the ICT skills: Students were made to work individually on those ICT skills. They were asked to explore the various parameters in as many ways as possible and draw out the maximum information.

Activity: The students were provided different activities to be done individually on their system.

Practice test: After the activity session the students were given a practice test on the concerned topic to determine their grasp on the content.

Encouragement: The learners were encouraged by the investigator.

Remediation: Appropriate remediation was provided by the investigator in running the ICT skill development program. Difficulties faced by the prospective teachers were resolved and they were made to undergo that ICT skill practice again.

Computer Achievement test: Once the chapter is completed, it was followed by a comprehensive test comprising of multiple choice and short answer type question. Practical tests were also taken.

4.1.5 VALIDATION OF ICT SKILLS DEVELOPMENT PROGRAM

In the process of validation the following steps were followed:-

1. Before the try-out of the package on prospective teachers, expert comment to improve the content organization and activities were taken from experts namely Dr Vidhi Bhalla, Assistant Professor, M.M college of Education, Mullana, Dr Rohit Bhandari, Assistant Professor, Dev Samaj College of education, Chandigarh, Dr. Harneet Billing, Indo Global College of Education, Abhipur,. Dr Vandana Sharma, Indo Global College of Education, Abhipur, Dr. Googi Gupta, Shivalik Institute of Education and Research, Mohali, Dr. S.P Ahuja, HOD, Department Computer Science and Dr. Prerna Joshi, Bhavan Vidyla, Panchkula.

2. The first Individual try out was done on 25 prospective teachers drawn from the Shivalik Institute of education and research, Mohali, Punjab.

3. Group try out was conducted on 50 prospective teachers of Pine Groove College of Education, Bassi Pathana, Distt. Fatehgarh Sahib, Punjab.

4. Certain inadequacies and discontinuity was found in the content of the instructional program. Thus to ensure effectiveness the learning material was revised by the investigator before proceeding further. Thus after careful revision, modifications were done and the tool was finalized.

4.2 COMPUTER SELF –EFFICACY SCALE BY EMBI (2007)

Computer self-efficacy scale by Embi (2007) was used in this study to measure an individual's perceptions of his capability regarding specific computer related knowledge and skills. The questionnaire was based on Durndell, Haag and Laithwaite's (2000) scale with slight modifications. In the pilot test, questionnaire was distributed among 20 faculty members at UITM in Malaysia. The overall reliability coefficient of the scale was .94. The instrument is comprised of 29 items consisting of three domains as shown in Table 4.1.

Table: 4.1: Distribution of items of computer self-efficacy scale in various domains

DOMAIN	ITEM NO.
BEGINNING SKILLS	1, 4, 5, 6, 9, 12, 14, 18, 20, 24
FILE AND SOFTWARE SKILLS	2, 15, 16, 17, 25, 27, 28
ADVANCED SKILLS	3, 7, 8, 10, 11, 13, 19, 21, 22, 23, 26, 29

4.2.1 Scoring

All the 29 items of the scale are positively worded items and are given a score of '1', '2', '3', '4' for strongly disagree, moderately disagree, moderately agree and strongly agree. The sum of these values gives the respondent's computer self-efficacy score. The total score varies from 29 to 116, showing least computer self-efficacy to highest computer self- efficacy. High score indicates respondents' high computer self- efficacy in using computers and vice-versa. For validation of the scale in Indian situations, the scale was administered randomly to 100 prospective teachers of Punjab
. Scoring was done according to specifications given. The total scores for the 100

prospective teachers were arranged in a descending order of the scores and 27% of the low scores and 27% of high scores were identified. Then, for each of the 29 items, a t- ratio was computed for the higher and the lower groups to find out the discriminating power of each item. t-ratio for each of the 29 items were found to be significant at
0.05 or 0.01 levels of confidence.

4.2.2 Reliability of the scale was estimated by test - retest method

The reliability of the test was determined by the test retest method. The test was administered to group of prospective teachers of Pine Groove College of Education, Bassi Pathana, Punjab and re administered to the same group after a gap of one month. The correlation between the scores was found to be 0.88 thus the reliability coefficient was 0.87. The value indicates that computer self efficacy scale is fairly reliable.

4.2.3 Validity

Face validity and content validity of the scale was ensured through consultation with experts from Panjab University, Chandigarh and Punjabi University, Patiala from the first draft till the final draft of the scale.

4.3 SELF REGULATION QUESTIONNAIRE BY BROWN, MILLER

& LAWENDOWSKI (1999)

Self regulation scale was developed specifically to study the self-regulatory processes, it describes meant to be general principles of behavioral self-control. The Self-Regulation Questionnaire (SRQ; (Brown, Miller, & Lawendowski, 1999) was developed as a first attempt to assess these self-regulatory processes through self- report. Items were developed to mark each of the seven sub processes of the Miller and Brown (1991) model, forming seven rationally-derived subscales of the SRQ. Subsequent analyses of the instrument have suggested that the scale contains one principal component, rather than specific factors corresponding to the rational subscales.

Self-regulation scale is the ability to develop, implement, and flexibly maintain planned behavior in order to achieve one's goals. Building on the foundational work of Frederick Kanfer (Kanfer, 1970a, 1970b).

1. Receiving relevant information
2. Evaluating the information and comparing it to norms

3. Triggering change
4. Searching for options
5. Formulating a plan
6. Implementing the plan
7. Assessing the plan's effectiveness

4.3.1 Reliability

Reliability of the SRQ appears to be excellent. In a community sample of 83 people with varying levels of self control, the SRQ was administered twice, separated by 48 hours, to test stability of scores it provides (Aubrey, Brown, & Miller, 1994). Test- retest reliability for the total SRQ score was high ($r = .94$, $p < .0001$). Internal consistency of the scale was also quite high (= .91), consistent with the idea that its items contain much redundancy.

4.3.2 Content Validity

The SRQ also has shown strong convergent validity with concomitant measures. In a sample of 300 college students (Brown, Baumann, Smith, & Etheridge, 1997), SRQ scores were inversely related to risk-taking ($r = -.244$, $p < .001$) and impulsivity.

4.3.3 Scoring

All 63 items are answered on a 5-point Likert scale with the following scale points:

Strongly disagree, Disagree, Uncertain or Unsure, Agree, Strongly Agree. For reverse-scaled items scores are as 1=5, 2=4, 3=3, 4=2 and 5=1.

    Above 239   High self regulation

    Between 214-238   Intermediate

    self regulation Below 213   Low

    self regulation

For validation of the scale in Indian situations, the scale was administered randomly to 100 prospective teachers from Punjab. Scoring was done according to specifications given. The total scores for the 100 prospective teachers were arranged in a descending order of the scores and 27% of the low scores and 27% of high scores were identified. Then, for each of the 63 items, a t-ratio was computed for the higher and the lower groups to find out the discriminating power of each item. T-ratios for each of the 63 items were found to be significant at 0.05 or 0.01 levels of confidence.

Reliability of the scale was estimated by test - retest method
The reliability of the test was determined by the test retest method. The test was administered to group of prospective teachers of Pine Groove College of Education, Bassi Pathana, Punjab and re administered to the same group after a gap of one month. The correlation between the scores was found to be 0.90 thus the reliability coefficient was 0.86. The value indicates that self regulation questionnaire is fairly reliable.

Validity

Face validity and content validity of the scale was ensured through consultation with experts from Panjab University, Chandigarh and Punjabi University, Patiala from the first draft till the final draft of the scale.

4.4 TECHNOLOGY INTEGRATION BELIEFS SCALE Step I: Planning of the Scale

While planning the scale the researcher followed Likert method of summated rating for construction of technology integration belief scale, so as to differentiate between more and less technology integration beliefs among prospective teachers. Statements formed were a mixture of positive and negative statements in order to add variety to the scale.

After discussion with experts, collected items were thoroughly screened and edited. 50 items pertaining to nine dimensions were included in the preliminary draft of scale. Out of the included 45 items, 37 items were positive and 8 were negative. The following points were kept in mind while writing the items.

I. Items were related to their dimension
II. Items were comprehensive to the respondent
III. The language of the items was such as that the respondent cam immediately identify with the situation expressed in the item.
IV. Those item were avoided that could be interpreted in more than one way or about which contradictions could arise.
V. The numbers of items developed were greater than to be retained in the scale.

Step II: - Preliminary form of Scale

After preliminary screening, editing of statement and their pre-try out modification the preliminary form of scale comprised of 45 items of Likert type on a five point rating scale. After careful exploration and survey of literature nine dimensions were taken such as:-

I. Value belief
II. Ethics
III. Constructivist belief
IV. Learner centered belief
V. Learning and teaching belief
VI. Use of ICT in class for teaching
VII. Preparation of printed material
VIII. Motivation to use technology
IX. Technology for communication

Technology integration belief scale is a five point scale. Every item is in statement form. Positive and negative statements are included in the scale to add variety and reduce the students' tendency to respond perfunctorily. Five response categories are provided for responding to each item. These response categories are

- Never

- Rarely
- Sometimes
- Mostly
- Always

Step III: Preparation of First Draft of the Scale

After careful exploration of literature, a pool of 45 items on different dimensions were written and edited. Out of the included 45 items, 38 were positive and 7 were negative. The following points were kept in mind while writing the items

(i) Items were related to their dimension
(ii) Items were comprehensive to the respondent
(iii) The language of the items was such that the respondent can immediately identify with the situation expressed in the item.

(iv) Those items were avoided that could be interpreted in more than one way or about which contradictions could arise.

(v) The number of items selected was greater than to be retained in the scale Distribution of items into four dimensions in the first draft is being presented in the table 4.2

Table 4.2: Distribution of dimension wise items of the first draft

1.	Value Belief	6	1,8,9,10,12,13
2.	Constructivist belief	4	14,15,19,27
3.	Learner centered belief	4	28,29,30,31
4.	Learning and teaching belief	6	32,33,42,43,44,45
5.	Use of ICT in class for teaching	9	3,16,17,18,20,21, 34, 36,37
6.	Preparation of printed material	5	2,4,5,6,38
7.	Motivation to use technology	3	7,35,39
8.	Technology use for communication	3	11,40,41
9.	Ethics	5	22,23,24,25,26

Step IV: Try- Out of the Scale

The first draft of 45 items was given to five experts for their valuable opinion. As the scale was to measure the attitude towards science, it was pertinent to choose judges from related field such as lecturers of schools, faculty members of university departments etc. The judges were told that they were free to add a relevant item and change or delete any item which they considered irrelevant and vague or not measuring the dimension under which they were put. The judges rendered their suggestions and views very frankly.

Step V: Item Analysis

Table 4.3: t- ratio for technology integration beliefs scales of the first draft

Item	t- ratio	Remarks	Item	t-ratio	Remarks
1	4.72	S	24	6.52	S
2	2.93	S	25	8.09	S
3	1.56	NS	26	3.78	S
4	5.21	S	27	4.96	S
5	5.42	S	28	5.57	S
6	4.99	S	29	3.92	S
7	3.92	S	30	7.04	S
8	5.17	S	31	3.14	S
9	7.34	S	32	2.97	S
10	4.24	S	33	7.35	S
11	1.17	NS	34	1.41	NS
12	5.33	S	35	2.43	NS
13	4.22	S	36	6.24	S
14	10.34	S	37	7.38	S
15	6.32	S	38	5.82	S
16	6.98	S	39	4.52	S
17	4.85	S	40	7.41	S
18	2.86	S	41	8.69	S
19	0.6	NS	42	5.29	S
20	4.16	S	43	9.67	S
21	6.58	S	44	8.54	S
22	5.93	S	45	9.18	S
23	6.33	S			

S= Significant, NS= Not significant

Table shows the t- ratio for item number 3, 11, 19 34 and 35 was not significant even at 0.05 level of significance and rest of the items were significant at 0.01 level of significance. Hence, 5 items were dropped and 40 items were retained for the final draft.

Step VI: Final form of the scale

The final form of the scale of scale consisted of 40 items out of which 33 were positive polarity and 7 items were of negative polarity.

Scoring

The scoring was done according to the scoring procedure suggested by Likert, (1932):

- Never   1
- Rarely   2
- Sometimes 3
- Mostly   4
- Always   5

For negative-scaled items, 1=5, 2=4, 3=3. 4=2 and 5=1

Step VII: Reliability of the Scale

The reliability of the test was determined by the test retest method. The test was administered to group of students Pine Groove College of Education, Bassi Pathana, Punjab and re administered to the same group after a gap of one month. The correlation between the scores was found to be 0.88 thus the reliability coefficient was 0.88. The value indicates that technology integration beliefs scale is fairly reliable.

Step VIII: Validity

Regarding method of establishing validity of questionnaire, It is necessary for the entire test to have content validity. Content validity is concerned with the relevance of contents of items, individually and as a whole. Each individual item or content of test should correctly and adequately measure the trait or variable in question and test as whole should contain only one representative type of the variable to be measured by the test. Face validity and content validity of the scale was ensured through consultation with experts from Panjab University, Chandigarh and Punjabi University, Patiala from the first draft till the final draft of the scale.

4.5 COURSE SATISFACTION QUESTIONNAIRE (CSQ) BY FREY, YANKELOV AND FAUL (2003)

CSQ is a 7-point Likert type self-report questionnaire which was developed by Frey, Yankelov and Faul (2003) to measure students' overall satisfaction with the computer courses. The contents include interaction between students and faculty, interaction among students, the relevancy of course content, and the teaching methods for delivering the content. It includes 21 items. Students were instructed to respond to the item from "completely dissatisfied" (1) to "completely satisfied" (7) with a possible range from 21 to 147. The higher scores represent more satisfaction with the courses. Frey et al. (2003) reported an internal consistency Cronbach' alpha equals to 0.97, indicating an excellent reliability. They also found that the CSQ scores moderately to strongly positively correlate with web-assisted strategies, such as communication, course information, learning resources, assignment, and grading. Course satisfaction questionnaire was administered to the participants at Auburn University (N=256).

4.5.1 Scoring

All the 21 items of the scale are positively worded items and are given a score of '1', '2', '3', '4','5', '6 and '7' for completely dissatisfied, mostly dissatisfied, somewhat dissatisfied, neither satisfied/dissatisfied, somewhat satisfied, mostly satisfied and completely satisfied. The sum of these values gives the respondent's course satisfaction. The total score varies from 21 to 147, showing least completely dissatisfied to highest completely satisfied.

4.5.2 Reliability and Validity

Frey et al. (2003) reported an internal consistency Cronbach' alpha equals to 0.97, indicating an excellent reliability. An exploratory factor analysis using a principal component extraction method and an albumin rotation of a 21-item self-report course satisfaction questionnaire was administered to the participants at Auburn University (N=256).

The Kaiser-Meyer-Olkin measure of sampling adequacy was 0.965, indicating that the present data were suitable for principal components analysis. Similarly, Bartlett's test of sphericity was significant (0.01), indicating sufficient correlation between the variables to proceed with the analysis. Using the Kaiser-Guttman retention criterion of eigen values greater than 1.0, a two-factor solution provided the clearest extraction accounting for 68.520% of the total variance. However, the score plot indicated a dominant factor with eigenvalues at 13.334 whereas the previous researchers only provided one structure for the Course Satisfaction Questionnaire. Therefore, one factor, Course Satisfaction, with 21-item was obtained. The corrected item-total

correlation ranged from 0.587 to 0.866, and the Cronbach's coefficient alpha was
0.970, which was corresponded to the original structure.

For validation of the scale in Indian situations, the scale was administered randomly to 100 prospective teachers of Pine Groove College of Education, Bassi Pathana, Punjab. Scoring was done according to specifications given. The total scores for the 100 prospective teachers were arranged in a descending order of the scores and 27% of the low scores and 27% of high scores were identified. Then, for each of the 21 items, a t-ratio was computed for the higher and the lower groups to find out the discriminating power of each item. t-ratios for each of the 21 items were found to be significant at 0.01 level of confidence.

Reliability of the scale was estimated by test - retest method
The reliability of the test was determined by the test retest method. The test was administered to group of prospective teachers and re administered to the same group after a gap of one month. The correlation between the scores was found to be 0.94. The value indicates that course satisfaction questionnaire is fairly reliable.

Validity

Face validity and content validity of the scale was ensured through consultation with experts from Panjab University, Chandigarh and Punjabi University, Patiala from the first draft till the final draft of the scale.

4.6 COMPUTER ACHEIVEMENT TEST

It has long been recognized that achievement tests are an integral and important part of educational process. It measures the extent to which a person has achieved acquired certain information or mastered certain skills, usually as a result of specific instruction (Stanley and Hopkins, 1978). Ebel (1966) was of the view that achievement test are a sample of indicator of a students' knowledge taken at a particular point of time. An achievement tests can be designed for two purposes. First, performance can be measured to provide information about the characteristics of student's present behavior. Second, achievement can be measured to provide information about the instructional treatment which produces that behavior. So from the above point of view the development of an achievement test was a crying need.

The planning of the test was done according to various aspects such as class, previous knowledge purpose of the test and subject matter included in the ICT skills development program. The investigator planned the test considering the following steps;

1. Planning
2. Preparation
3. Try-out and
4. Evaluation.

Table4.4: Blue print of specification of achievement test (First draft)

S.N	Level of Cognitive Domain	T/F	Blank	Diagram	MCQ	Match	Total
1	Knowledge	7	10	3	36	2	58
2	Comprehension	7	7	2	20	1	37
3	Application	3	6	3	09	2	23
	Total	17	23	8	65	5	118

4.6.1 First draft of Computer achievement test

The preliminary draft of the achievement test was constructed. This was discussed with Dr Vidhi Bhalla, Assistant Professor, M.M college of Education, Mullana, Dr Rohit Bhandari, Assistant Professor, Dev Samaj College of Education, Chandigarh Dr. Harneet Billing, Indo Global College of Education, Abhipur,. Dr Vandana Sharma, Indo

Global College of Education, Abhipur, experts in the area who critically appraised each item. On the basis of suggestion of subject matters experts, 28 items were dropped. These were considered to be either redundant of irrelevant or had language ambiguity. Thus, 90 item were retained for the first try- out of the test.

First try out of computer achievement test and item analysis
In order to ensure that the entire class of learner behaviours had been circumscribed a try out was conducted. The first draft of computer achievement test was administered to a sample of 100 prospective teachers drawn from the B.Ed of Pine Groove Collage of Education, Bassi Pathana and Punjab who had already covered the content of the test. Normal testing condition was ensured to the prospective teachers. After the test was completed by all the prospective teachers, the paper were collected and scored

with help of scoring key developed by the investigator. Each item response marked correctly by the students was given one mark. No correction for guessing was applied as very negligible percentage of students made omission. Stanley and Hopkins (1972) along with (1996) have suggested the application of correction for guessing when some students have omitted a fairly large number of items.

After the scoring, the item-analysis of the test was carried out. The items were analyzed qualitatively, in terms of their content, form and quantitatively in terms of their statistical properties. For this all the scored answer sheets were selected with highest scores and the same number with lowest scores were selected to form upper and lower groups (Kelley, 1939). For the calculation of discriminatory value and difficulty value the following procedure was followed:

(i) The answer sheets of all the students were arranged in descending order.
(ii) The top 27% formed the upper group and bottom 27% formed lower group.
(iii) After that the correct responses for each item in both the groups were calculated

Each group consisted of 27 students. As such difficulty value and discriminatory power were calculated from those sub groups making a total of 54 students. For calculating difficulty value and discriminatory power following formulae were used:

$$D.V. = \frac{R_U + R_L}{N}$$

$$D.P. = \frac{R_U - R_L}{0.5 N}$$

Where:

R_U = Number of right responses in the upper group. R_L = Number of right responses in the lower group. N = Total number of students in both the groups.

Table 4.5: Difficulty value and discriminating powers of the items in the draft of computer achievement test

Item	R_U	R_L	D.V.	D.P.		Item	R_U	R_L	D.V.	D.P.	
1	24	19	0.80	0.19	R	46	17	11	0.52	0.22	A
2	20	12	0.59	0.30	A	47	23	15	0.70	0.30	A
3	13	6	0.35	0.26	A	48	25	21	0.85	0.15	R
4	25	15	0.74	0.37	A	49	18	11	0.54	0.26	A
5	17	10	0.50	0.26	A	50	19	12	0.57	0.26	A
6	17	10	0.50	0.26	A	51	23	11	0.63	0.44	A
7	27	23	0.93	0.15	R	52	27	18	0.83	0.33	A
8	13	5	0.33	0.30	A	53	18	11	0.54	0.26	A
9	22	15	0.69	0.26	A	54	21	10	0.57	0.41	A
10	22	16	0.70	0.22	A	55	21	15	0.67	0.22	A
11	22	16	0.70	0.22	A	56	25	15	0.74	0.37	A
12	22	14	0.67	0.30	A	57	23	14	0.69	0.33	A
13	19	12	0.57	0.26	A	58	23	20	0.80	0.11	R
14	27	22	0.91	0.19	R	59	21	13	0.63	0.30	A
15	17	11	0.52	0.22	A	60	22	15	0.69	0.26	A
16	18	11	0.54	0.26	A	61	25	15	0.74	0.37	A
17	21	15	0.67	0.22	A	62	20	13	0.61	0.26	A
18	23	17	0.74	0.22	A	63	27	22	0.91	0.19	R
19	21	17	0.70	0.15	R	64	19	12	0.57	0.26	A

20	20	13	0.61	0.26	A	65	25	10	0.65	0.56	A
21	20	14	0.63	0.22	A	66	22	16	0.70	0.22	A
22	14	8	0.41	0.22	A	67	15	9	0.44	0.22	A
23	21	15	0.67	0.22	A	68	15	8	0.43	0.26	A
24	24	19	0.80	0.19	R	69	24	16	0.74	0.30	A
25	17	10	0.50	0.26	A	70	23	17	0.74	0.22	A
26	19	13	0.59	0.22	A	71	25	15	0.74	0.37	A
27	22	15	0.69	0.26	A	72	23	17	0.74	0.22	A
28	15	9	0.44	0.22	A	73	27	23	0.93	0.15	R
29	16	8	0.44	0.30	A	74	22	16	0.70	0.22	A
30	18	11	0.54	0.26	A	75	23	17	0.74	0.22	A
31	27	25	0.96	0.07	R	76	21	15	0.67	0.22	A

32	23	10	0.61	0.48	A	77	24	10	0.63	0.52	A
33	27	22	0.91	0.19	R	78	20	15	0.65	0.19	A
34	21	14	0.65	0.26	A	79	26	10	0.67	0.59	A
35	19	14	0.61	0.19	R	80	25	21	0.85	0.15	R
36	20	13	0.61	0.26	A	81	21	15	0.67	0.22	A
37	19	13	0.59	0.22	A	82	25	20	0.83	0.19	R
38	20	14	0.63	0.22	A	83	21	15	0.67	0.22	A
39	22	15	0.69	0.26	A	84	25	15	0.74	0.37	A
40	23	14	0.69	0.33	A	85	20	14	0.63	0.22	A
41	23	14	0.69	0.33	A	86	25	16	0.76	0.33	A
42	23	13	0.67	0.37	A	87	15	9	0.44	0.22	A
43	23	18	0.76	0.19	R	88	16	7	0.43	0.33	A
44	19	10	0.54	0.33	A	89	21	13	0.63	0.30	A
45	23	13	0.67	0.37	A	90	25	20	0.83	0.19	R

Note: Here 'A' stands for accepted and 'R' stands for rejected

The selection of items was done according to Ebel's criteria (1966. Table shows the

distribution of computer achievement test as per Ebel's discriminating power.

Table 4.6: distribution of discriminating powers of the items

of first draft of computer achievement test after first try out

S. No.	D.P.		Remarks
1	0.40 and above	35	Very good items
2	Between 0.30 and 0.39	22	Reasonably good items
3	Between 0.20 and 0.29	18	Needs improvement
4	0.19 and below	15	Very Poor items
	Total	90	

Second try out and item analysis

In revised draft of achievement test was again administered to a sample of 100 students of who had already studied the content. Once again the difficulty values of each item were calculated. The major reason for measuring item difficulty was to choose items of suitable difficulty level. The criteria given by Ebel (1996) say that having difficulty level above 0.75 and below 0.25 was rejected as they were very easy and very difficult respectively. The items having difficulty value between 0.25 to 0.75 were accepted as such for the achievement test. However the difficulty level of first draft ranged from 0.54 to 0.96.

Table 4.7 : Distribution of discriminating power of items of the first draft of computer achievement test after second try-out

S. No.	D.P.	Question	Remarks
1	0.40 and above	33	Very good items
2	0.30 - 0.39	15	Reasonably good items
3	0.20 - 0.29	12	Marginal items
4	0.19 and below	-----	Poor items
	Total	60	

Table shows that 33 items having discriminating power more than 0.40 were considered as very good items, 15 items with D.P. between 0.30 to 0.39 were considered considerably good items, 12 items with value between 0.20 to 0.29 were regarded as marginal items while 15 items having D.P. between 0.19 and below deserved to be eliminated.

Table 4.8: Blue print of final draft of computer achievement test

Units	Knowledge	Comp	App	Total
Computer and its components	3	2	2	7
Introduction to MS word	2	2	1	5
Editing formatting text in MS word	5	4	2	11
Creating & formatting table in MS word	2	4	1	7
Printing	1	1	2	4
Starting to MS power point	1	1	1	3
Slide transition & animation	4	2	0	6

Adding formatting text in MS PowerPoint	2	4	1	7
Internet	3	2	2	7
Use of Skype	1	1	1	3
Total		24	23	13	60

4.6.2 SCORING

The scoring procedure followed for the final draft has been given below

- All the items carry equal marks
- For each correct response a score of 1 was assigned and zero for the incoresct response.
- There was no negative marking
- Maximum marks for the test were 60

4.6.3 RELIABILITY OF THE ACHIEVEMENT TEST

Reliability concerns the extent to which measurement are repeatable, i.e. when different people make the measurement on different occasions, with supposedly alternative instruments for measuring the same thing (Nunnally,1982). In other words, measurement is intended to be stable over a variety of conditions in which essentially the same results should be obtained.

For determining the reliability of the achievement test, it was administered to 75 students of Punjab at two different occasions. Test-retest coefficient of correlation was computed which was found to be 0.88. Ebel (1966) suggests that most test constructors are satisfied when their test yield reliability coefficient in the vicinity of 0.90. Reliability coefficient of the present test was 0.88. Therefore, computer achievement test may be considered a reliable tool for measurement of the student's computer achievement.

4.6.4 VALIDITY

Content Validity was determined by showing that the behaviors demonstrated in testing constitute a representative sample of performance domain. The domain usually involves learned knowledge and skills. Thus, it is commonly used for achievement test (Wolf, 1982). The content validity is determined by comparing the items in a test with the content and objectives of a particular domain to see how well they match, as it is content of a particular direction. For the present test, content validity was determined on the basis of the coverage of the content. The test represents a fairly well-defined universe of content, content was made closely parallel to the tasks constituting the universe under study and performance on individual items was determined both with respect to the accuracy of the responses and the process used to solve the items.

CHAPTER V
METHOD OF THE STUDY

A theoretical framework of variables, significance of problem, development, related literature and description of the tools have been discussed. The present chapter focuses on the sample, design of the study, procedure, the operational definitions of the terms used in the study and statistical techniques employed. The method of the study has been discussed under following headings:

- 5.1 Design of the study
- 5.2 Selection of sample
- 5.3 Selection of Tools used
- 5.4 Procedure followed
- 5.5 Statistical technique used for data analysis
- 5.6 Precaution observed
- 5.7 Constraints and difficulties faced during the experiment

5.1 DESIGN OF THE STUDY

Research methodology plays an important role in any research process. It describes the various steps involved in solving research problem. A research design is a detailed plan of the investigation. In fact, it is the detailed procedure of testing the hypotheses and analyzing the obtained data. Experimental method of research was employed for the present study as this method is aimed at establishing cause and effect relationship between variable under study through some systematic and well planned observation carried out in controlled conditions.

Table 5.1: Diagrammatic Presentation of the Study

Group	Independent Variable	Outcome before treatment	Outcome after treatment	Difference in outcomes	Net Effect (Gain)
Experimental	ICT skill development Program	E1	E2	E= E2-E1	E-C
Control	Traditional teaching method	C1	C2	C=C2-C1	

Where

E = Gain measure of experimental group C= Gain measure of control group

E1= Measure of outcome of the experimental group before the treatment C1= Measure of outcome of the control group before the treatment

E2= Measure of outcome of the experimental group after the treatment C2= Measure of outcome of the control group after the treatment

Variable undertaken for the study

In the present experiment study, the variables undertaken were:

INDEPENDENT VARIABLE

It comprised of:

1. Information and communication technology skills development program
2. Traditional method of instruction

DEPENDENT VARIABLE

It comprised of:

1. Self regulation
2. Computer self efficacy

3. Technology integration beliefs
4. Course outcomes with respect to computer achievement and satisfaction

The above variables were measured twice during the course of the study: first before the treatment i.e., pre-test stage and then after completing the experimental treatment i.e., at the post-test stage.

5.2 SELECTION OF SAMPLE

For the current investigation, the population was the prospective teachers of education colleges of Punjab. A sample of prospective teachers was purposively selected. The procedure of selecting the sample given below.

Prospective teachers of education colleges and sample distribution

The sample was selected at two levels for education colleges and prospective teachers viz.

(i) Bachelor of Education (B.Ed) college sample

(ii) Prospective teachers sample

(i) Bachelor of Education (B.Ed) college sample

Based on the criteria of permission from college principal regarding conducting experimental study, two education colleges were chosen for the study viz.

Table 5.2: College wise distribution of sample

S. NO.	NAME OF COLLEGE
1.	Indo Global College of Education, Abhipur, Distt. Mohali
2.	International Divine College of Education, Ratwara sahib Mullanpur

Prospective teacher sample

From the selected two private education colleges, 102 prospective teachers were randomly chosen from two private education colleges. The colleges were compared with regards to the criteria that college has almost same classroom climate, physical facilities, teacher taught ratio, sex ratio, digital lab etc.

Table 5.3: Distribution of Students According to the treatment

S. NO	NAME OF GROUP	STUDENTS
1.	Control Group	51

2.	Experimental Group	51
	Total	102

Fig 5.1: DIAGRAMMATIC PRESENTATION OF THE STUDY

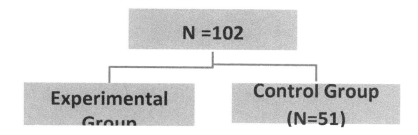

5.3 SELECTION OF TOOLS

The following tools were used for collecting data:

Tools are the techniques which are appropriate for the collection of certain types of evidence or information for conducting the research. The tools used for the present study are given below:

1. Information and Communication Technology (ICT) skills development program (Developed by investigator).
1. Computer Self Efficacy Scale (Cassidy & Eachus, 2002)
2. Self Regulation Scale (Brown, Miller, & Lawendowski, 1999)
3. Technology integration beliefs scale (Developed by the investigator)
4. Course outcomes test viz.
    5.1 Computer achievement (Developed by investigator)
    5.2 Course Satisfaction Questionnaire (Frey, Yankelov and Faul, 2003).

5.4 PROCEDURE FOLLOWED

Phase I:

Selecting the Sample

The sample was selected as explained under the sub heading sample.

Phase II: Pre-testing phase

This phase will involve administration of the following test to the prospective teachers of experimental and control groups:

- Computer self efficacy test
- Self regulation test
- Technology integration beliefs scale
- Course outcomes viz.
    - Computer achievement test
    - Satisfaction

Phase III: Instructional treatment phase

The experimental group was exposed to information and communication technology skills development program and control group was exposed to traditional instruction for thirty five sessions of forty minutes duration. Both groups were taught similar topics, but were exposed to different instructional treatments. The topics were taken from the computer application paper of B.Ed syllabus under Punjabi university, Patiala. The students in the two groups are mentioned in the table below:

Table 5.4: List of student for experimental and control group for experimental treatment

S.No	Experimental group	Control group
1.	Tanika Gupta	Aditi
2.	Sakshi Sharma	Amanjeet Kaur
3.	Sakshi Arora	Anjali Rani
4.	Neha Jaswal	Ankur
5.	Jasleen	Anu Sidhu
6.	Mandeep	Ekta
7.	Neha Sharma	Gagandeep Kaur
8.	Jyoti Sharma	Harleen Kaur
9.	Jyoti	Harmeet Kaur
10.	Gaurav Sharma	Jyoti
11.	Kanwal Pal Singh	Kajalrani
12.	Fatehdin	Karamjeet Kaur
13.	Jaswinder Kaur	Kirandeep Kaur
14.	Nitu	Manpreet Kaur
15.	Amandeep	Meena Doda
16.	Bharti Jangpo	Mamta Sharma
17.	Anju Thakur	Neha Tomar

18.	Narinder	Pallavi
19.	Vinod Kumar	Parveen Bano
20.	Harneet Kaur	Priyanka Bist

21.		Gurmeet Kaur	Ritu Sidhu
22.		Jatinder Kaur	Sobia
23.		Rajwinder Kaur	Paminder Kaur
24.		Anshi Chandra	Vasu Kausal
25.		Parminder Kaur	Pardeep Kaur
26.		Diksha Saini	gurdeep kaur
27.		Ramandeep Kaur	Preeti Verma
28.		Ankita Singh	Sonia Rani
29.		Renuka Joshi	Mandeep Kaur
30.		Gurpreet Kaur	Gurjeet Singh
31.		Priyanka Gulati	Parshant Sharma
32.		Anu Gupta	Preeti Verma
33.		Rinku Rani	Vasu Kaushal
34.		Shruti Singh	Sharn Kaur
35.		Kiran	Ritu Sidhu
36.		Gurbhej Kaur	Ramnik Kaur
37.		Sandeep Kaur	Rajesh Bala
38.		Sandeep Kaur	Poonamjot Kaur
39.		Parwinder Kaur	Ravneeet Kaur
40.		Kulbir	Shivani Sharma
41.		Ranjot Kaur	Pardeep Kaur
42.		Parkash Singh	Meenakshi Mangla
43.		Vasudha Jain	Navjot Singh
44.		Reena	Naurhi

| 45. | Harmanjit Kaur | Nishan Singh |

46.	Shelly Sapra	Samiksha Sood
47.	Navraj Kaur	Ruby
48.	Pooja Verma	Sanjeevan Kaur
49.	Amarpreet Kaur	Ramnik Kaur
50.	Reeta	Ravinder Kaur
51.	Isha Sharma	Rama Rani

EXPERIMENTAL GROUP STUDENTS WORKING IN THE COMPUTER BASED INSTRUCTIONAL SETUP

During the computer used study, the students worked on individual computers for 35 sessions of 40 minutes duration each. The steps followed for the experimental treatment were:

- Students were introduced to program in the digital classrooms. Appropriate orientation was given with the objectives of using computer as a mode of instruction.
- Students were taught and trained to use program and its various components
- The topics related to the content were taught by investigator in digital classroom before using the computers.
- During the course of each session, the students accessed the software i.e. ICT skills development program on their individual systems and worked on it.

- The topics related to the content were taught by investigator in digital classroom before using the computers.
- Appropriate care was taken to motivate students to go through study material of the relevant chapter again. The exercises were reattempted by the students to improve their performance.
- During the entire exercise the investigator facilitated and made sure that each student worked smoothly on their system on their own pace.
- The investigator evaluated the performance of each student in the practice session.
- After each session the students were encouraged for better performance in the next sessions.

- It was ensured that the experiment was carried out in a disciplined environment with the students working independent of each other.
- The students were also encouraged to save energy by turning off their computers after each session.

CONDUCTING THE PRACTICE TEST

- In order to measure the understanding of the students on the concerned content, practice exercise were administered after the instructional treatment. Each lesson of ICT skills development program was followed by practice exercise. It was ensured that the content and length of the practice exercise was in accordance with the material taught in the instructional material phase using interactive simulations.
- The students of control group were taught by traditional instructional method.

Scoring

The scoring of the students was done by the investigator on the basis of their performance and feedback was given.

Phase IV: Post-Testing

After completion of instructional program of thirty five sessions of forty minute duration each, the following test was again administered to both experimental and control groups:

- Computer self efficacy test
- Self regulation test
- Technology integration beliefs
- Course outcomes viz.
    - Computer achievement test
    - Satisfaction

5.5 SCHEDULE OF EXPERIMENT Pre-Testing

Date wise schedule for the administration of the pre test of the experimental study for both the groups

11th March 2015 - Administration of self regulation questionnaire to both groups 12th March 2015 - Computer achievement test to both the groups

13th March 2015 - Administration of computer self efficacy and technology integration beliefs scale to both the groups

Table 5.5: Details of conduct of Information and Communication Technology Skill Development Instructional Programme

S. NO	GROUP	NAME OF THE COLLEGE
1.	Experimental Group	**Indo Global College of Education, Abhipur, Distt Mohali**
2.	Date Schedule	14th March 2015 to 24th April 2015
3.	Control Group	**International Divine College of Education, Ratwara Sahib Mullanpur**
4.	Date Schedule	14th March 2015 to 24th April 2015

Control Group

The same content was taught to control group by traditional instructional method on the same dates.

Post -Testing

Date Wise Schedule for the Administration of Post Test for Experimental and Control Group

25th April 2015 - Administration of self regulation questionnaire to both groups 27th April 2015 - Computer achievement test to both the groups

28th April 2015 - Administration of computer self efficacy and technology integration beliefs scale to both the groups

29th April 2015 - Course Satisfaction Questionnaire to both the groups

5.6 STATISTICAL TECHNIQUES USED

The following statistical techniques have been employed to analyze the data obtained from the experiment in order to test the hypotheses.

(i) Descriptive statistics techniques viz, mean, standard deviation, skewness and kurtosis were used to determine the nature of distribution of the scores.
(ii) Graphical presentations were used for visual perception of the data.
(iii) t-test was employed for testing the significance of difference between the mean gain scores of different groups on variables under study.

5.7 PRECAUTIONS OBSERVED

While conducting the experimental study, certain precautions were observed so as to control experimental conditions with high precision and effectiveness. The precautions taken were:

- The sample was chosen from the education colleges of same level i.e. affiliated to same university.
- The investigator taught both the experimental and control group to avoid any variation in the instructional process.
- It was ensured that the students were not under kind of stress undue control throughout the study to avoid artificiality in their behavior.
- Orientations were carried out with the students before actually carrying out the program to establish rapport with them.
- Discussions were carried out to understand the problem faced by them while studying internet and Skype.
- Teaching period of 40 minutes duration was completely utilized for the treatment.
- It was ensured that the experimental group was administered instruction on individual computers not

in groups.
- Effort was made by the investigator to avoid any kind of artificiality in

    students' behaviour by providing equal attention to both the groups.
- Prospective teachers were provided enough time and freedom to express themselves and be comfortable with the variety of activities during experimentation.
- Due care was given to prepare the ICT skills development program by appropriately fitting the content matter into it.

5.8 Constraint and difficulties faced during the experiment

Every task is accompanied with some constraints and difficulties. Few of them to mention were:

- Digital lab with internet facility
- Power Backup
- Time table related difficulties
- Class management during the experimental session
- Digital classroom

Sufficient efforts were needed to convince the administration, principal, teachers about the importance of the experimental to make them agree to cooperate in the experiment. The authorities were contacted and briefed about the program and its usefulness. It is the essential requisite that the treatment should be fully provided to every student. The time table in-charges were contacted for making some changes in the regular time table. Despite these constraints the researcher carried out the experiment very smoothly.

GLIMPSES OF INFORMTATION AND SKILL DEVELOPMENT PROGRAM

INTERACTION AMONG STUDENTS AND INVESTIGATOR

PROSPECTIVE TEACHERS WITH INVESTIGATOR IN DIGITAL LAB

PROSPECTIVE TEACHERS WITH INVESTIGATOR IN CLASSROM

PROSPECTIVE TEACHERS WITH INVESTIGATOR IN DIGITAL LAB DURING LAB SESSION

PROSPECTIVE TEACHERS WITH INVESTIGATOR IN DIGITAL LAB

PROSPECTIVE TEACHERS WITH INVESTIGATOR IN DIGITAL LAB

CHAPTER – VI

ANALYSIS OF DATA AND INTERPRETATION OF RESULTS

The most critical part of any study is analysis of data. The statistical analysis of the data not only enables the researcher to test the hypotheses, but also to interpret the data, draw conclusions and to make generalizations as well. The present chapter deals with analysis of the data, interpretation and discussion of the results. In the preceding chapters, the problem of the study, objectives, hypotheses, development and description of the tools and the procedure of the experiment were discussed. The data was analyzed through computer using SPSS 20 package. Accordingly, the relevant statistical techniques like mean, standard deviation and t-test were worked out for testing of the hypotheses.

The data obtained from the experimental study has been analysed by categorising into the following headings:

6.1 Analysis of mean gain scores on computer self efficacy

6.2 Analysis of mean gain scores of self regulation

6.3 Analysis of mean gain scores of technology integration beliefs

6.4 Analysis of mean gain scores of course outcome in

relation to computer achievement

6.5 Analysis of mean scores of course outcome in relation to course satisfaction.

As mentioned in the previous chapter, treatment was the independent variable. There were four dependent variable, namely, computer self efficacy, self regulation, technology integration beliefs and course outcomes with respect to computer achievement and course satisfaction.

Independent variable

Instructional Treatment

- ❖ Experimental Group: Exposed to Information and Communication Technology Skills Development Program
- ❖ Control Group : Exposed to Conventional / Traditional method

Dependent Variable

The effect of instructional treatment i.e. ICT Skills Development Program was studied with respect to the following four dependent Variables:

- Computer self efficacy
- Self regulation
- Technology integration beliefs
- Course outcome with respect to computer achievement and course satisfaction

6.1 ANALYSIS OF MEAN GAIN SCORES ON COMPUTER SELF EFFICACY

In a pre test – post test design, it is essential to ascertain that both groups selected for study are equal. For this purpose, the investigator administered the computer self efficacy scale on both experimental and control group and result of the same has been given in table 6.1. The computer self efficacy scores were analysed using descriptive statistics which involves mean and Standard Deviation. t-test was employed on the pre-test scores of the treatment groups on computer self efficacy.

Table 6.1: t-ratio for the pre-test computer self efficacy

scores of experimental and control group

Dimensions	Treatment	Mean	S.D	t-ratio	Remarks
Beginning skills	Control	26.84	3.27	0.70	Not Significant
	Experimental	26.31	3.74		
File and software skills	Control	17.45	3.61	1.87	Not Significant
	Experimental	18.75	3.35		
Advanced skills	Control	26.61	3.61	1.08	Not Significant
	Experimental	25.82	3.69		
Computer Self Efficacy	Control	69.9	6.07	1.94	Not Significant
	Experimental	71.49	6.48		

** Significant at 0.01 level; * Significant at 0.05 level

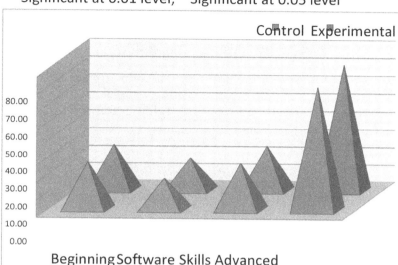

Fig 6.1: A bar diagram depicting comparison of mean of pre-test scores on computer self efficacy

It may be observed from table 6.1 and fig 6.1 that the t- ratio in difference of mean pre-test scores on computer self efficacy for dimension 'Beginning skills' of the experimental and control group is.76, which in comparison to the table value was not found to be significant even at 0.05 level of significance. The result indicates that the two groups were not different on 'Beginning skills'.

It may be observed from the table 6.1 and Fig 6.1 that the t ratio in difference of mean pre-test scores on computer self efficacy for dimension 'File and Software Skills' of the experimental and control group is 1.88, which in comparison to the table value was not found to be significant even at 0.05 level of significance. The result indicates that the two groups were not different on 'File and Software Skills'.

It may be observed from the table 6.1 and fig 6.1 that the t-ratio in difference of mean pre-test scores on computer self efficacy for dimension 'Advanced Skills' of the experimental and control group is 1.08, which in comparison to the table value was not found to be significant even at 0.05 level of significance. The result indicates that

the two groups were not different on 'Advancing Skill'.

Further it is apparent from table that computed t- ratio came out to be 1.92 for the mean difference of computer self efficacy on overall skills. The computed t ratio is not significant at 0.05 level of significance. The result indicates that the two groups were not different on computer self efficacy before the treatment. Thus it was inferred that the two treatment groups were comparable with regard to their previous knowledge.

Comparison of Pre-Test and Post-Test Mean Scores of Experimental and Control Group on Computer Self Efficacy

The dimension wise pre-test and post-test mean scores of students falling into two groups were subjected to descriptive statistics Mean, Standard Deviation, Skewness and Kurtosis were calculated. The obtained pre-test and post-test scores on computer self efficacy for experimental and control groups have been given in table 6.2.

Table 6.2: A summary of Descriptive statistics for computer self efficacy scores of experimental

Dimensions	Experimental Group	N	Mean	S.D	Skew	Kurt
Beginning Skills	Pre Test	51	26.31	3.74	-0.24	-1.06
	Post Test	51	36.12	3.09	-0.49	-0.88
File and Software Skills	Pre Test	51	18.75	3.35	0.5	0.23
	Post Test	51	25.49	1.94	-0.29	0.28
Advanced Skills	Pre Test	51	25.82	3.69	-0.08	-0.2
	Post Test	51	41.16	3.3	-0.88	1.92
Computer Self Efficacy	Pre Test	51	71.49	6.48	-0.16	-0.13
	Post Test	51	102.76	5.05	-0.52	0.87

To substantiate the data presented in table 6.2, 6.2(a), a bar diagram has been drawn to depict the difference in mean pre-test and post-test scores on beginning skills, file and software skills, advanced skills and computer self efficacy for experimental and control group before and after the instructional treatment is given in fig 6.2(a).

Table 6.2(a): A summary of Descriptive statistics for computer self efficacy scores of Control group

Dimensions	Control Group	N	Mean	S.D	Skew	Kurt
Beginning Skills	Pre Test	51	26.84	3.27	0.14	-0.2
	Post Test	51	29.78	5.54	-0.54	-0.2
File and Software Skills	Pre Test	51	17.45	3.61	-0.31	-0.57
	Post Test	51	20.25	3.59	-0.4	0.34
Advanced Skills	Pre Test	51	26.61	3.61	0.41	-0.27
	Post Test	51	28.67	3.49	-0.38	0.54
Computer Self Efficacy	Pre Test	51	69.9	10.9	-0.32	-0.46
	Post Test	51	78.7	9.4	-0.19	-0.4

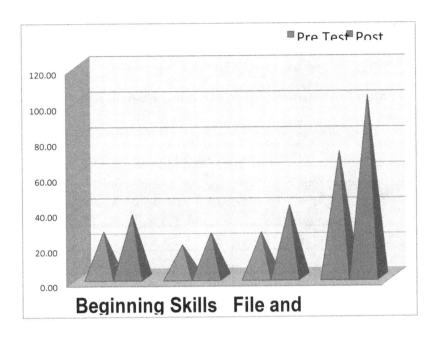

Fig 6.2: Bar diagram depicting difference in mean scores on

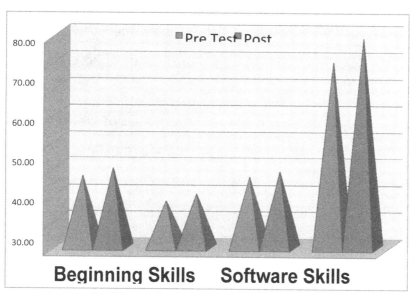

computer self efficacy for Experimental group

Fig 6.3: A bar diagram depicting comparison in mean scores on computer self efficacy for control group

Skewness is measure of the symmetry of the probability distribution of real valued random variable about its mean. For a unimodal distribution, negative skewness indicates that the tail on the left side of the probability density function is longer than the right side. Conversely, positive skewness indicates that the tail is on the right is longer that the left side. The value of skewness lies within the acceptable limits of normality of distribution i.e.±1. While kurtosis is a measure of data is peaked or flat relative to the normal distribution. Distribution with negative or positive excess kurtosis is called platykurtic or leptokurtic distribution respectively. The value of kurtosis lies within the acceptable limits of normality of distribution i.e.±1.96.

It may be revealed from the table 6.2 that values of skewness and kurtosis of the experimental and control group lied in the acceptable limits. It was found that the value of skewness lied within the acceptable limits of normality of distribution i.e.±1 and thus the distribution of the measure between pre-test and post-test scores may be considered as normal. The analysis of table 6.2 shows that post test scores of experimental group shows a platykurtic distribution with a flatter peak and values widely spread around mean whereas the pre- test score are highly peaked values.

COMPARISON OF MEAN GAIN SCORES OF EXPERIMENTAL AND CONTROL GROUP ON COMPUTER SELF EFFICACY

Further, the mean gain scores (Post test – Pre-test) were obtained and data analysis was conducted on gain scores. The Mean, Standard Deviation and t-ratio were calculated.

The following sets of null hypotheses were tested through this analysis:

H1 There is no significant difference in the mean gain scores on the computer self efficacy of prospective teachers exposed to different instructional treatments.

Further hypothesis were formulated to analyse mean difference on computer self efficacy with respect to the three domains.

The two instructional treatments yield equal mean difference scores on: $H_{1.01}$ Beginning skills

$H_{1.02}$ File and Software skills $H_{1.03}$ Advanced Skills

Table 6.3: t-ratio for mean gain scores of experimental and control group on computer self efficacy

Dimensions	Group	N	Mean	S.D	t-ratio	Remarks
Beginning Skills	Experimental	51	9.81	4.78	5.89**	Significant
	Control	51	2.8	7.14		
File and Software Skills	Experimental	51	6.74	3.09	5.43**	Significant
	Control	51	2.07	5.38		
Advanced Skills	Experimental	51	15.34	4.11	14.25**	Significant
	Control	51	2.94	4.79		
Computer Self Efficacy	Experimental	51	33.37	7.76	18.45**	Significant
	Control	51	8.8	5.95		

** Significant at 0.01 level; * Significant a 0.05 level

Analysis Of Data and Interpretation Of Result

Mean Gain Scores: From the table 6.3 it was observed that mean gain of experimental group was 33.37 and of control group were 8.8. This shows that the gain in computer self efficacy scores was higher for the experimental groups than the control group.

Standard Deviation: The table 6.3 reveals that for experimental group imparted instruction through ICT skill

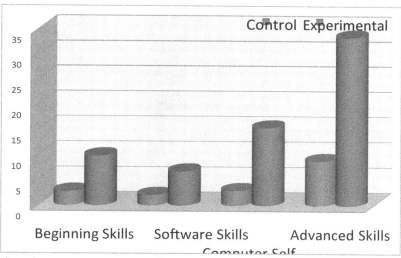

Computer Self

development program i.e. experiment group the standard deviation was 7.76 and of control group was 5.95. This shows that the gain scores on computer self efficacy for the two treatment groups were well distributed.

Fig 6.4: Bar diagram showing comparison in gain scores of experimental and control group on various dimensions of computer self efficacy

Beginning Skills

It may be observed from the table 6.4 and Figure 6.3 that the t-ratio in difference of mean gain score on computer self efficacy for dimension 'Beginning Skills' of the experimental and control group is 5.09, which in comparison to the table value was found to be significant even at 0.01 level of significance. It shows that there is significant difference in the mean gain scores of experimental and control group. Hence, the null hypothesis $H_{1.01:}$ There is no significant difference in the mean gain scores on computer self efficacy with respect to Beginning Skills of the two groups, was rejected. The result indicates that the two groups were different on 'Beginning Skills' after the experimental treatment. Hence, it may be inferred that the experimental group exhibited better mean gain score on "Beginning skills" than control group after the instructional treatment. An examination of mean gain scores indicates that ICT skill development program were superior to conventional method.

File and Software Skills

It may be observed from the table 6.4 and fig. 6.3 that the t-ratio in difference of mean gain scores on computer self efficacy for dimension 'File and Software Skills' of the experimental and control group is 5.33, which in comparison to the table value was found to be significant at 0.01 level of significance. It shows that there is difference in the mean gain scores of both groups. Hence, the null hypothesis $H_{1.02}$: There is no significant difference in mean gain scores on computer self efficacy with respect to 'File and Advancing Skill' of the two groups, was rejected. The result indicates that the two groups were different on 'File and Software Skills' after the experimental treatment. It shows that the experimental group exhibited better mean gain score on 'File and Software Skills' than control group after the instructional treatment.

Advanced Skills

It may be observed from the table 6.4 and fig 6.3 that the t-ratio in difference of mean gain scores on computer self efficacy for dimension 'Advanced Skills' of the experimental and control group is 12.54, which in comparison to the table value was found to be significant even at 0.01 level of significance. It shows that there is difference in the mean gain scores. Hence, the null hypothesis $H_{1.03}$: There is no significant difference in the mean gain scores on computer self efficacy with respect to 'Advanced Skills' of the two groups, was rejected. The result indicates that the two groups were different on 'Advanced Skills' after the experimental treatment. It shows that the experimental group exhibited better mean gain score on 'Advancing Skills' than control group after the instructional treatment.

Computer Self Efficacy

Further it is apparent from table 6.4 that computed t ratio came out to be 13.89 for the difference in mean gain scores of computer self efficacy. The computed t- ratio is significant at 0.01 levels of significance. Hence, the null hypothesis H_1: There is no significant difference in the mean gain scores on computer self efficacy, was rejected. The result indicates that the two groups were different on computer self efficacy after the experimental treatment. It shows that the experimental group exhibited better mean gain score on computer self efficacy than control group after the instructional treatment.

6.1.1 DISCUSSION OF RESULTS OF COMPUTER SELF EFFICACY SCORES

The present study revealed that there is significant difference in the mean gain scores on the computer self efficacy of prospective teachers exposed to different instructional treatments. Thus, H1 was rejected as the t- ratio for the difference in the mean gain scores in computer self efficacy of the two treatment groups was found to be highly significant at 0.01 level of significance.

The result in agreement with the finding that computer self efficacy is enhanced by the teaching through ICT skills development program, online learning, CBI, CBMI, and web based learning as compared to traditional instruction. This is supported by the researches on computer self efficacy by Anderson and Maninger, 2007; Ocak and Akdemir, 2008; Liaw, 2008; Saade and Kira, 2009; Teo, 2009; Tantrarungroj & Suwannatthachote , 2012. Several studies have demonstrated the effect of computer anxiety and computer self-efficacy on computer related behaviors. Computer self-efficacy has been shown to be positively related to performance during computer training (Webster & Martocchio, 1992). A student's confidence about computer skills may affect the willingness to learn about computer skills. The less confident a student feels about computer skills, the more he or she desires to learn about computer technology (Zhang & Espinoza, 2004). Computer self-efficacy was also found to be associated with attitudes toward computer technologies (Zhang & Espinoza, 1998). Furthermore, Zhang and Espinoza (1998) also reported that past enrolment in computer programming courses was found to be positively related to self-efficacy and computer self-efficacy positively related to plans to take more computer related courses. A high level of computer anxiety, on the other hand, has been negatively related to learning computer skills (Harrington, McElroy, & Morrow, 1990), resistance to the use of computers (Torkzadeh & Angula, 1992; Weil & Rosen, 1995), and poorer task performance (Heinssen et al., 1987). Research on computer self- efficacy in general also revealed that males on average have better computer self- efficacy than females (Torkzadeh & Koufteros, 1994). Seferoglu (2007) examined the perceptions of students in the faculty of education regarding their self efficacy in relation to computer use. Results also indicate that participants' gender is significantly related with their computer self efficacy in relation to some specific aspects.

$H_{1.01}$ was rejected as the t ratio for the mean gain scores of computer self efficacy with respect to 'Beginning Skills' found to be significant at 0.01 level of significance. The result indicates that the two groups were different on 'Beginning Skills' when taught through two instructional treatments.

$H_{1.02}$ was rejected as the t-ratio for the mean gain scores of computer self efficacy with respect to 'File and Software Skills' found to be significant at 0.01 level of significance. The result indicates that the two groups were different on 'File and Software Skills' when taught through two instructional treatments.

$H_{1.03}$ was rejected as the t ratio for the mean gain scores of computer self efficacy with respect to 'Advanced Skills' found to be significant at 0.01 level of significance. The result indicates that the two groups were different on 'Advanced Skill' when taught through two instructional treatments.

6.2 ANALYSIS OF MEAN GAIN SCORES OF SELF REGULATION

The analysis of pre-test self regulation scores was analysed using descriptive statistics which involve mean, standard deviation. t-test was employed on the pre- test scores of the treatment groups on self regulation scores. The obtained pre - test scores on self regulation for Experimental and control groups have been given in table 6.4.

Table 6.4: t-ratio for the pre-test score of experimental and control group on self regulation

Dimensions	Group	N	Mean	S.D	t-ratio	Remarks
Receiving	Control	51	25.69	4.17	1.25	Not Significant
	Experimental	51	24.61	4.48		
Evaluating	Control	51	27.1	4.45	1.41	Not Significant
	Experimental	51	25.48	3.46		
Triggering	Control	51	26.08	3.90	0.92	Not Significant
	Experimental	51	25.37	3.77		
Searching	Control	51	27.02	5.17	1.61	Not Significant
	Experimental	51	25.49	4.19		
Formulating	Control	51	25.10	4.62	1.38	Not Significant
	Experimental	51	26.29	3.42		
Implementing	Control	51	25.10	4.10	1.21	Not Significant
	Experimental	51	26.07	3.89		
Assessing	Control	51	26.16	3.99	0.26	Not Significant
	Experimental	51	25.92	4.81		
	Control	51	182.45	14.97		

Self Regulation					1.01	Not Significant
	Experimental	51	179.43	13.83		

** Significant at 0.01 level; * Significant at 0.05 level

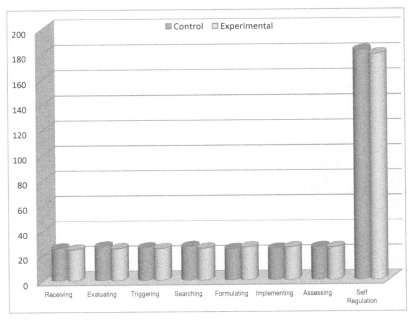

Fig 6.5: Bar diagram showing comparison of mean pre-test scores of experimental and control group on self regulation

It may be observed from the table 6.4 and figure 6.5 that the t-ratio in difference of mean pre-test scores of experimental and control group on self regulation for dimensions 'Receiving, Evaluating, Triggering, Searching, Formulating, Implementing and assessing are 1.25, 1.41, 0.92, 1.61, 1.38, 1.21, and 0.26 which in comparison to the table value was not found to be significant even at 0.05 level of significance.

The result indicates that the two groups experimental and control group are almost same on various dimensions of self regulation.

Comparison of Pre-Test and Post-Test Mean Scores of Experimental and Control Group on Self Regulation

The dimension wise pre-test and post-test mean scores of students falling into two groups were subjected to descriptive statistics Mean, Standard Deviation, Skewness and Kurtosis were calculated. The obtained pre-test and post-test scores on self regulation for experimental and control groups have been given in table 6.5.

Table 6.5: A summary of Descriptive statistics of experimental group on pre-test and post-test scores on self regulation

Dimensions	Experimental	N	Mean	S.D	Skew	Kurt
Receiving	Pre test	51	24.61	4.48	-0.06	0.24
	Post test	51	29.27	4.07	-0.26	-1.16
Evaluating	Pre test	51	25.48	3.46	0.38	1.03
	Post test	51	29.2	4.39	-0.94	0.65
Triggering	Pre test	51	25.37	3.77	-0.47	1.45
	Post test	51	29.41	4.53	-0.95	0.84
Searching	Pre test	51	25.49	4.19	-0.41	0.45
	Post test	51	30.84	3.64	-0.7	-0.13
Formulating	Pre test	51	26.29	3.42	-0.92	1.05
	Post test	51	30.88	3.03	-0.42	-0.28
Implementing	Pre test	51	26.07	3.89	0.18	0.98
	Post test	51	30.80	4.00	-0.83	-0.33
Assessing	Pre test	51	25.92	4.81	-0.3	1.49
	Post test	51	30.73	3.77	-0.54	-0.94
Total	Pre test	51	179.43	13.83	0.45	-0.02
	Post test	51	211.65	18.98	-0.71	-0.51
Dimensions	Control	N	Mean	S.D	Skew	Kurt
Receiving	Pre test	51	25.69	4.17	-0.47	0.58
	Post test	51	26.02	2.92	-0.58	0.24
Evaluating	Pre test	51	27.10	4.45	-0.48	1.95
	Post test	51	27.88	2.88	-0.29	0.18
Triggering	Pre test	51	26.08	3.90	0.19	0.98
	Post test	51	26.73	3.35	0.12	-0.29
Searching	Pre test	51	27.02	5.17	-0.21	0.74
	Post test	51	27.80	3.36	0.13	0.42

Formulating	Pre test	51	25.10	4.62	-0.08	0.27
	Post test	51	27.00	2.94	0.26	-0.07
Implementing	Pre test	51	25.10	4.1	-0.52	0.75
	Post test	51	24.8	3.47	0.35	0.64
Assessing	Pre test	51	26.16	3.99	-0.01	0.86
	Post test	51	27.25	3.3	-0.26	-0.63
Self Regulation	Pre test	51	182.45	14.97	0.07	-0.14
	Post test	51	188.92	7.92	-0.65	0.47

** Significant at 0.01 level; * Significant at 0.05 level

Analysis Of Data and Interpretation Of Result

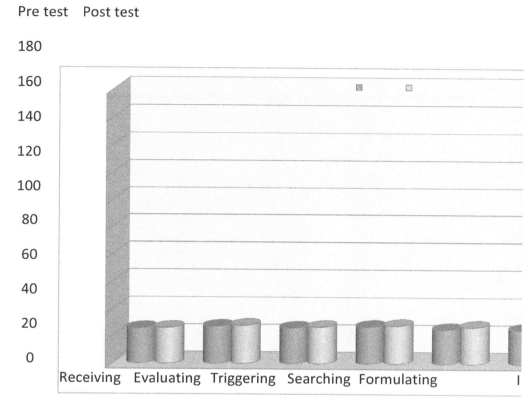

Fig 6.6: Bar diagram showing mean of Pre-test and post- test scores of control group on various dimensions of self regulation

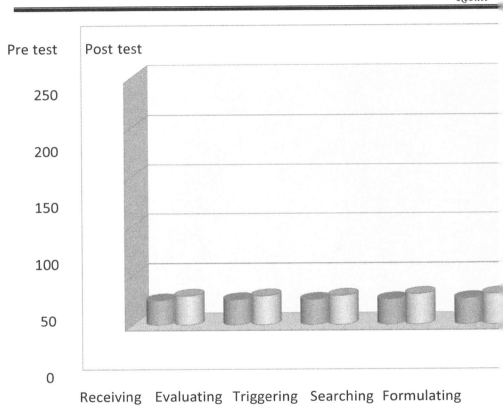

Fig 6.7: Bar diagram showing mean of Pre-test and post-test scores of experimental group on various dimensions of self regulation

To substantiate the data presented in table 6.5, a bar diagram has been drawn to depict the dimension wise difference in mean pre-test and post-test scores on receiving, evaluating, triggering, searching, formulating, implementing, assessing and self regulation for experimental and control group before and after the instructional treatment in fig 6.6 and 6.7.

It can be observed from table 6.6 and Fig.6.7 that value of Pre-test and post-test mean scores experimental group is comparable, while it is almost same for control group. The mean value of post-test is higher for experimental group. The value of S.D is almost equal for two groups. Further it can also be observed that the mean pre-test and post test scores of experimental group on overall self regulation are 188.92 and
211.65. The result indicates that the two groups were different on the variable after treatment.

It may be revealed from the table 6.6 that values of skewness of the experimental and control group lied in the acceptable limits. It was found that the value of skewness lied within the acceptable limits of normality of distribution i.e.±1 and thus the distribution of the measure between pre-test and post-test scores may be considered as normal. The analysis of table 6.6 shows that post-test scores of experimental group shows a mesokurtic with a flatter peak and values widely spread around mean whereas the pre-test score are highly peaked values whereas in control group the curve is leptokurtic for post-test scores.

COMPARISON OF MEAN GAIN SCORES OF PROSPECTIVE TEACHERS ON SELF REGULATION

Further, the mean gain scores (Post test – Pre-test) were obtained and data analysis was conducted on gain scores. The Mean, Standard Deviation and t-ratio were calculated.

The following set of Null Hypotheses was tested through this analysis:

H2   There is no significant difference in the mean gain scores on self regulation of prospective teachers exposed to different instructional treatments.

Further hypothesis were formulated to analyse mean difference on Self Regulation with respect to the seven domains.

The two instructional treatment yield equal mean difference scores on: $H_{2.01}$ Receiving

H₂.₀₂ Evaluating H₂.₀₃
Triggering   H₂.₀₄
Searching   H₂.₀₅
Formulating   H₂.₀₆
Implementing   H₂.₀₇
Assessing

Table 6.6: Significance of difference between mean gain scores of experimental and control group on self regulation

Dimensions	Group	Mean	S.D	t-ratio	Remarks
Receiving	Control	0.33	4.86	4.01**	Significant
	Experimental	4.67	5.98		
Evaluating	Control	0.78	5.03	2.36*	Not Significant
	Experimental	3.22	5.48		
Triggering	Control	0.65	4.76	3.25**	Significant
	Experimental	4.04	5.79		
Searching	Control	0.78	5.99	3.97**	Significant
	Experimental	5.35	5.74		
Formulating	Control	1.9	4.93	3.18**	Significant
	Experimental	4.8	4.35		
Implementing	Control	0.29	5.08	4.46**	Significant
	Experimental	4.73	5.91		

Assessing	Control	1.1	5.21	3.39**	Significant
	Experimental	4.8	5.88		
Self Regulation	Control	5.25	16.18	6.80**	Significant
	Experimental	32.12	23.15		

** Significant at 0.01 level; * Significant at 0.05 level

Analysis Of Data and Interpretation Of Result

Mean Gain Scores: From the table 6.6 it was observed that mean gain of experimental group was 32.12 and of control group were 5.25. This shows that the gain in self regulation scores was higher for the experimental group than the control group.

Standard Deviation: The table 6.6 reveals that for experimental group imparted instruction through ICT skill development program

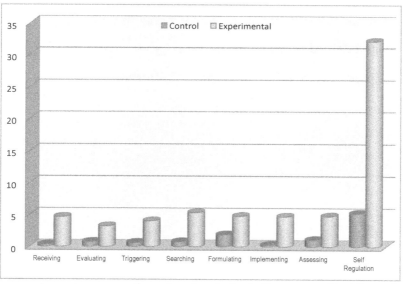

i.e. experiment group the standard deviation was 23.15 and of control group was 16.18. This shows that the gain scores on self regulation for the two treatment groups were well distributed.

Fig 6.8: Bar diagram showing comparison of mean gain scores of experimental and control group on various dimensions of self regulation

Receiving

It is evident from the table 6.6 and fig 6.8 that the mean gain scores of experimental and control group on "Receiving" dimension of SRQ were 4.67 and 0.33 along with their SD's 5.98 and 4.94 respectively. The compared t-ratio came out to be 4.01 which is more than the required table values at 0.01 level of significance and hence significant. Hence, the null hypothesis $H_{2.01}$: There is no significant difference in the mean gain scores on self regulation of prospective teachers exposed to different instructional treatments with respect to "Receiving', was rejected. The result indicates

that the two groups were different on 'Receiving' after the experimental treatment.

Evaluating

It is evident from the table 6.6 that the mean gain scores of experimental and control

group on "Evaluating" dimension of SRQ were 3.22 and 0.78 along with their SD's

5.48 and 5.03 respectively. The compared t-ratio came out to be 2.36 which is significant at 0.05 level of significance. Hence, the null hypothesis $H_{2.02}$: There is no significant difference in the mean gain scores on self regulation of prospective teachers exposed to different instructional treatments with respect to "Evaluating', was rejected. The result indicates that the two groups were different on 'Evaluating'. It shows that the experimental group exhibited better mean gain score on dimension 'Evaluating' than control group after the instructional treatment.

Triggering

It is evident from the table 6.6 that the mean gain scores of experimental and control

group on "Triggering" dimension of SRQ were 4.04 and 0.65 along with their SD's

5.79 and 4.76 respectively. The compared t- ratio came out to be

3.25 which is more than the required table values at .01 level of significance and hence significant. Hence, the null hypothesis $H_{2.03}$ There is no significant difference in the mean gain scores on self regulation of prospective teachers exposed to different instructional treatments with respect to "Triggering', was rejected. The result indicates that the two groups were different on 'Triggering'. It shows that the experimental group exhibited better mean gain score on dimension 'Triggering' than control group after the instructional treatment.

Searching

It is evident from the table 6.6 that the mean gain scores of experimental and control group on "Searching" dimension of SRQ were 5.35 and 0.78 along with their SD's 5.74 and 5.99 respectively. The compared t ratio came out to be 3.97 which is more than the required table values at 0.01 level of significance and hence significant. Hence, the null hypothesis $H_{2.04}$: There is no significant difference in the mean gain scores on self regulation of prospective teachers exposed to different instructional treatments with respect to "Searching', was rejected. The result indicates that the two groups were different on 'Searching'. It shows that the experimental group exhibited better mean gain score on dimension 'Searching' than control group after the instructional treatment.

Formulating

It is evident from the table 6.6 that the mean gain scores of experimental and control

group on "Formulating" dimension of SRQ were 4.88 and 1.9 along with their SD's

4.35 and 4.93 respectively. The compared t ratio came out to be 3.18 which is more than the required table values at 0.01 level of significance and hence significant. Hence, the null hypothesis $H_{2.05}$: There is no significant difference in the mean gain scores on self regulation of prospective teachers exposed to different instructional treatments with respect to "Formulating', was rejected. The result indicates that the two groups were different on 'Formulating'. It shows that the experimental group exhibited better mean gain score on dimension 'Formulating' than control group after the instructional treatment.

Implementing

It is evident from the table that the mean gain scores of experimental and control group on "Implementing" dimension of SRQ were 4.73 and 0.29 along with their SD's 5.91 and 5.08

respectively. The compared t ratio came out to be 4.46 which is more than the required table values at .01 level of significance and hence significant. Hence, the null hypothesis $H_{2.06}$: There is no significant difference in the mean gain scores on self regulation of prospective teachers exposed to different instructional treatments with respect to 'Implementing', was rejected. The result indicates that the two groups were different on 'Implementing'. It shows that the experimental group exhibited better mean gain score on dimension 'Implementing' than control group after the instructional treatment.

Assessing

It is evident from the table 6.6 that the mean gain scores of experimental and control group on "Assessing" dimension of SRQ were 4.8 and 1.1 along with their SD's 5.88 and 5.21 respectively. The compared t-ratio came out to be 3.39 which is significant at 0.01 level of significance and hence significant. Hence, the null hypothesis $H_{2.07}$: There is no significant difference in the mean gain scores on self regulation of prospective teachers exposed to different instructional treatments with respect to 'Assessing', was rejected. The result indicates that the two groups were different on 'Assessing'. It shows that the experimental group exhibited better mean gain score on dimension 'Assessing' than control group after the instructional treatment.

Self regulation

Further it can also be observed that the mean post test scores of experimental and control group on self regulation were 32.12 and 5.25 with corresponding SD's 23.18 and 16.15 respectively. The computed t-value came out to be 6.80 which is significant at 0.01 level of significance. Hence, the null hypothesis H2: There is no significant difference in the mean gain scores on scores on self regulation of prospective teachers exposed to different instructional treatments, was rejected. The result indicates that the two groups were different on self regulation after the treatment. It shows that the experimental group exhibited better mean gain score on Self Regulation than control group after the instructional treatment.

6.2.1 DISCUSSION OF RESULTS OF SELF REGULATION SCORES

H2 was rejected as the t-ratio for the difference in the mean gain scores in self regulation of prospective teachers exposed to different instructional treatment was found to be highly significant at 0.01 levels of significance. On all dimensions of self regulation, the students of experimental group exhibited better gain scores than control group.

The result is in agreement with the finding that self regulation is enhanced by the teaching through ICT skills development program, online learning, CBI, CBMI, and web based learning etc. as compared to traditional instruction. This is supported by the researches on self regulation Azevedo, 2005; Convergent empirical results have also been found that endorse the idea that the reason for these difficulties is that students do not deploy self-regulating processes while learning (Azevedo, Cromley, & Seibert, 2004; Graesser, McNamara, & VanLehn, 2005; Quintana, Zhang, & Krajcik, 2005). (i.e., Boekaerts & Corno, 2005; Brophy, 2004; De la Fuente, Pichardo, Justicia, & Berbén, 2008; Elliot, 2008; Moskowitz & Grant, 2009; Nunez, Solano, Gonzalez-Pienda, & Rosario, 2006; Riggs & Gholar, 2009; Schunk & Zimmerman, 2008; Zimmerman, 2008), the great challenge that faces us may be to build and test instructional models that support and promote SRL within contexts that are full of new information technologies (Cardelle-Elawar & Sanz de Acedo, 2010; Perry, Hutchinson, & Thauberger, 2008). Previous research results suggested that self- regulated learning affected course satisfaction and performance (Artino & McCoach, 2008; Puzziferro, 2008). The results of this study supported previous findings.

$H_{2.01}$ was rejected as the t- ratio for the mean gain scores of self regulation with respect to 'Receiving' found to be significant at 0.01 levels of significance. The result indicates that the experimental and control group were different on 'Receiving' when exposed to two instructional treatments.

$H_{2.02}$ was rejected as the t- ratio for the mean gain scores of self regulation with respect to 'Evaluating' found to be significant at 0.05 level of significance. The result indicates that the experimental and control group were different on 'Evaluating' when exposed to two instructional treatments.

$H_{2.03}$ was rejected as the t- ratio for mean gain scores of self regulation with respect to 'Triggering' found to be significant at 0.01 level of significance. The result indicates that the experimental and control group were different on 'Triggering' when exposed to two instructional treatments.

$H_{2.04}$ was rejected as the t- ratio for the mean gain scores of self regulation with respect to 'Searching' found to be significant at 0.01 level of significance. The result indicates that the experimental and control group were different on 'Searching' when exposed to two instructional treatments.

$H_{2.05}$ was rejected as the t- ratio for the mean gain scores of self regulation with respect to 'Formulating' found to be significant at 0.01 level of significance. The result indicates that the experimental and control group were different on 'Formulating' when exposed to two instructional treatments.

$H_{2.06}$ was rejected as the t- ratio for the mean gain scores of self regulation with respect to 'Implementing' found to be significant at 0.01 level of significance. The result indicates that the experimental and control group were different on 'Implementing' when exposed to two instructional treatments.

$H_{2.07}$ was rejected as the t-ratio for the mean gain scores of self regulation with respect to 'Assessing' found to be significant at 0.01 levels of significance. The result indicates that the experimental and control group were different on 'Assessing' when exposed to two instructional treatments. On all dimensions of self regulation, the students of experimental group exhibited better gain than control group.

6.3 ANALYSIS OF MEAN GAIN SCORES IN TECHNOLOGY INTEGRATION BELIEFS

The analysis of technology integration beliefs score was done using descriptive statistics which involves mean, standard deviation and inferential statistics which include test of significance. The obtained pre-test scores on technology integration beliefs for Experimental and control groups have been given in table 6.7

Table 6.7: t-ratio for the difference in the pre test mean scores of experimental and control groups on technology integration beliefs

Group	N	Mean	S.D	t-ratio	Remarks
Experimental	51	89.29	7.06	0.40*	Not Significant
Control	51	88.65	8.89		

** Significant at 0.01 level; * Significant at 0.05 level;

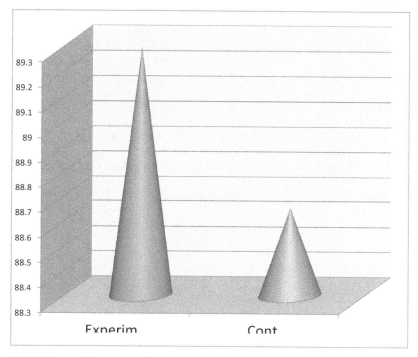

Fig 6.9: Bar diagram showing comparison of mean scores of experimental and control group on technology integration beliefs

It may be observed from the table 6.7 and Fig 6.9 that the t-ratio in difference in the mean scores of experimental and control group before experimental treatment is 0.40. This calculated t value is not significant at 0.05. Therefore, it could be interpreted that there is no significant difference in the mean scores of experimental and control group on technology integration beliefs before the experimental treatment i.e. both the groups are almost similar with respect to their scores in pre-test.

Comparison of Pre-Test and Post-Test Mean Scores of Experimental and Control Group on Technology Integration Beliefs

The pre-test and post-test mean scores of students falling into two groups were subjected to descriptive statistics Mean, Standard Deviation, Skewness and Kurtosis were calculated. The obtained pre-test and post-test scores on technology integration beliefs for experimental and control groups have been given in table 6.8.

Analysis Of Data and Interpretation Of Result

Table 6.8: A summary of Descriptive statistics for technology integration beliefs control group and experimental group

Control Group	N	Mean	S.D	Skew	Kurt
Pre test	51	88.65	8.89	0.32	-0.45
Post test	51	94.18	7.32	0.24	-0.21
Experimental Group	N	Mean	S.D	Skew	Kurt
Pre test	51	89.29	7.06	-0.46	0.27
Post test	51	172.45	6.94	0.94	1.69

From the table 6.8, it can be inferred that that the distribution is positively skewed for both the experimental and control group with a longer tail towards the right side as compared to left side. The

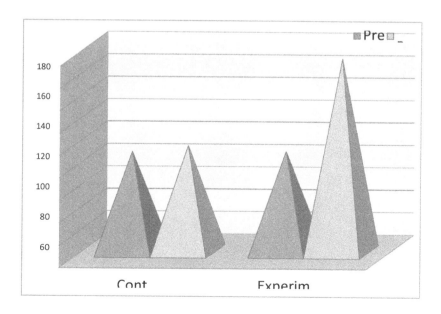

distribution for the experimental group is platykurtic in nature with a positive value whereas the control group is leptokurtic in nature with negative value.

Fig 6.10: Bar diagram showing comparison of mean scores of experimental and control group on technology integration beliefs

It is evident from the table 6.8 and fig. 6.10 that the two instructional treatments yield different mean scores in technology integration beliefs. It shows that prospective teachers taught through ICT skills development program showed higher mean in technology integration beliefs as compared to those taught through conventional method. Therefore, it could be interpreted that there is significant difference in the mean score of experimental group on technology integration beliefs after the experimental treatment i.e. both the groups are not similar with respect to their scores in after the instructional treatment.

COMPARISON OF MEAN GAIN SCORES OF EXPERIMENTAL GROUP AND CONTROL GROUP ON TECHNOLOGY INTEGRATION BELIEFS

Further, the mean gain scores (Post test – Pre-test) were obtained and data analysis was conducted on gain scores. The Mean, Standard Deviation and t-ratio were calculated.

The following Null Hypothesis was tested through this analysis:

H3 There is no significant difference in the mean gain scores on technology integration beliefs of prospective teachers exposed to different instructional treatments.

The analysis of gain score was analysed using t- test. The obtained t-value on technology integration beliefs for Experimental and control groups has been given in table 6.9.

Table 6.9: t - ratio for difference in mean gain scores of experimental and control group on technology integration beliefs

Group	N	Mean	S.D	t-ratio	Remarks
Control	51	5.53	7.32		
Experimental	51	83.16	11.01	42.19**	Significant

** Significant at 0.01 level; * Significant at 0.05 level

Mean Gain Scores: From the table 6.9 it was observed that mean gain of experimental group was 83.16 and of control group were 5.53. This shows that the gain in technology integration beliefs was higher for the experimental groups than the control group.

Standard Deviation: The table 6.9 reveals that for experimental group imparted instruction through ICT skill development program

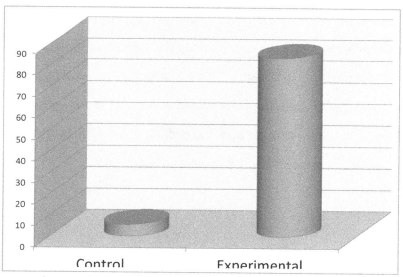

i.e. experiment group the standard deviation was 11.01 and of control group was 7.32. This shows that the gain scores on technology integration beliefs for the two treatment groups were well distributed.

Figure 6.11: Bar diagram showing comparison of Means Gain Scores of Experimental and Control Groups on technology integration beliefs

As shown in the table 6.9, t-value for the difference in the mean gain scores of experimental and control group after experimental treatment is 42.19. This calculated t- value is significant at 0.01 level of significance. Therefore, it could be interpreted that there is significant difference in the mean gain scores of experimental and control group on technology integration beliefs after the experimental treatment i.e. both the groups are different with respect to their mean gain scores. Hence, the null hypothesis H4: There is no significant difference in the mean gain scores on technology integration beliefs of the two groups, was rejected. The result indicates that the two groups were different on technology integration beliefs. Hence, it can be inferred from table that experimental group exhibited better mean gain scores than control group on technology integration belief after the experimental treatment.

6.3.1 DISCUSSION OF RESULTS OF TECHNOLOGY INTEGRATION BELIEFS

H3 was rejected as the t-ratio for the difference in the mean gain scores in technology integration beliefs of prospective teachers exposed to different instructional treatment was found to be highly significant at 0.01 levels of significance. (Helsel DeWert & Levine Cory, 1998; McKenzie, 2001; Saylor & Kehrhahn, 2003; Wasser & McNamara, 1998; Christensen, 2002) revealed that teachers' competence with computer technology is a key factor of effective use of ICT in teaching. Peralta and Costa (2007) conducted a study on 20 teachers' competences and confidence regarding the use of ICT in classrooms. They revealed that in Italy, teachers' technical competence with technology is a factor of improving higher confidence in the use of ICT. Many researchers investigate different aspects of technology integration beliefs and supported that technology integration plays important in prospective teachers curriculum(Kotrlik & Redmann, 2005; Bauer and Kenton, 2005; Judson, 2006; Totter
;2006; ChanLin, 2006; Zhao, 2007; Gulbahar, 2007; Anderson and

Maninger, 2007; Abbit and Klett, 2007; & Wood and Ashfield, 2008)

6.4 ANALYSIS OF MEAN GAIN SCORES ON COMPUTER ACHIEVEMENT

In order to compare and determine the significance between the means of achievement score of pre- test of experimental group and control group t value was computed. In a pre test – post test control group design, it is essential to ascertain that both groups selected for study are equal. For this purpose, the investigator administered the computer achievement test on both experimental and control group and result of the same has been given in table.

Table 6.10: t- ratio for mean pre test score of experimental and control group on computer achievement

Group	N	Mean	S.D		Remarks
Control	51	17.64	4.01		Not Significant
Experimental	51	19.82	5.12	1.15	

** Significant at 0.01 level; * Significant at 0.05 level

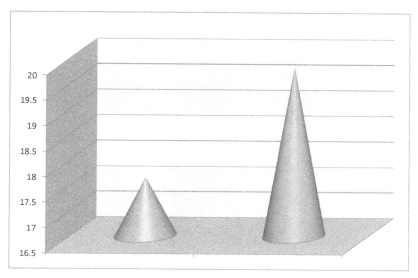

Figure 6.12: Bar diagram showing comparison of Means Pre-test Scores of Experimental and Control Groups on computer achievement test

It can be observed from table 6.10 and figure 6.12 that the mean scores of the experimental and control groups on computer achievement are 17.64 and 19.82 with corresponding SD's 4.01 and 5.12 respectively. The calculated t-value was found to be 1.15 which is less than the required table value at 0.05 level of significance. So, it is not significant. It means that there is no significant difference between the pre-test scores of experimental and control group on computer achievement test score. So, it can be inferred that both groups are almost similar with respect to their achievement scores in pre-test.

Comparison of Pre-Test and Post-Test Mean Scores of Experimental and Control Group on Computer Achievement

The pre-test and post-test mean scores of students falling into two groups were subjected to descriptive statistics Mean, Standard Deviation, Skewness and Kurtosis were calculated. The obtained pre-test and post-test scores on computer achievement for experimental and control groups have been given in table 6.5.

Analysis Of Data and Interpretation Of Result

Table 6.11: A summary of Descriptive statistics for Computer Achievement

Group	Computer Achievement	N	Mean	S.D	Skew	Kurt
Experimental	Pre Test	51	19.82	6.86	0.52	0.42
	Post Test	51	53.11	3.85	1.00	1.52
Control	Computer Achievement	N	Mean	S.D	Skew	Kurt
	Pre Test	51	17.64	4.01	0.18	-0.51
	Post Test	51	22.94	5.03	0.29	1.33

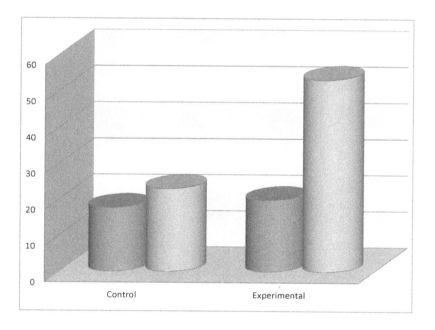

Figure 6.13: Bar diagram showing comparison of means Pre-test

and post-test Scores on computer achievement test

It is evident from the table 6.11 and fig. 6.13 that the two instructional treatments yielded different mean scores in computer achievement. It shows that prospective teachers taught through ICT skills development program showed higher computer achievement as compared to those taught through conventional method. Therefore, it could be interpreted that there is significant difference in the mean score of experimental group on computer achievement after the experimental treatment i.e. both the groups are not similar with respect to their scores in computer achievement.

It may be revealed from the table 6.11 that values of skewness and kurtosis of the experimental and control group lied in the acceptable limits. It was found that the value of skewness lied within the acceptable limits of normality of distribution i.e. ±1 and thus the distribution of the measure between pre-test and post-test scores may be considered as normal. The analysis of table 6.11 shows that post test scores of experimental group shows a platykurtic distribution with a flatter peak and values widely spread around mean whereas the pre- test score are highly peaked values.

COMPARISON OF MEAN SCORES OF EXPERIMENTAL AND CONTROL GROUP ON COMPUTER ACHIEVEMENT

Further, the mean gain scores (Post test – Pre-test) were obtained and data analysis was conducted on mean gain scores. The Mean, Standard Deviation and t-ratio were calculated.

The following Null Hypotheses was tested through this analysis:

H4   There is no significant difference in the mean gain scores on course outcomes of prospective teachers exposed to different instructional treatments with respect to computer achievement.

The gain scores was analysed using t- test. The obtained t-value on computer achievement for Experimental and control groups has been given in table

Table 6.12: t - ratio for difference in mean gain scores of experimental and control group on Computer Achievement

Group	N	Mean	S.D	t- ratio	Remarks
Experimental	51	33.29	7.80	23.52**	Significant
Control	51	5.30	2.54		

** Significant at 0.01 level; * Significant at 0.05 level

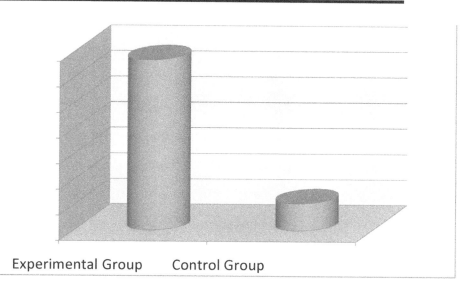

Figure 6.14: Bar diagram showing comparison Mean Gain Scores of Experimental and Control Groups on Computer Achievement

It is apparent from the table 6.12 and figure 6.14 t-value for difference in the mean gain scores of control and experimental group are 23.52 which is significant at 0.01 level of significance on computer achievement. Therefore, there exists significant difference in the mean gain scores on computer achievement of prospective teachers exposed to different instructional treatments. The mean gain scores of experimental group (33.29) are better than control group (6.35). It indicates that instructional treatment has good effect on the experimental group. Hence, the null hypothesis H4: There is no significant difference in the mean gain scores on computer achievement of the two groups, was rejected. The result indicates that the two groups were different on computer achievement after the experimental treatment. It shows that Experimental group taught through ICT skills development program showed higher computer achievement as compared to control group taught through conventional method.

6.4.1 DISCUSSION OF RESULTS OF COMPUTER ACHIEVEMENT

H4 was rejected as the t ratio for the difference in the mean scores in computer achievement of prospective teachers exposed to different instructional treatment was found to be highly significant at 0.01 levels of significance. Despite the potential advantages of ICT use, the impacts of ICT on learning outcomes have not shown consistent results (Aristovnik, 2012; Shaikh, & Khoja, 2011). British Educational Communications and Technology Agency BECTA (2000) performed a study looking into the correlation between educational performance and access and usage of Information and Communication Technology (ICT) in British schools. The study used: English, mathematics, and science test scores. 2,500 primary schools in England participated in the study. For the analysis, schools were divided into ICT resource categories. In English, BECTa (2000) used the 1999 grades from national tests. They found that primary schools with 'Very Good' ICT resources were significantly more likely to gain good grades on the national tests. Rockman et al. (2000) investigated the impact of laptop computers on students' and teachers' attitude and performance in schools. Students in certain American schools were provided with their own personal laptop computers. The researchers found that the use and access to laptops had a broad positive effect on both students and teachers. Angrist et al. (2001) found no evidence of a relationship between CAI and test scores. Tremblay et al. (2001) which found no relationship between the presence of a computer in the classroom and the achievement of third grade students. Kulik's (1994) meta-analysis study revealed that, on average, students who used ICT-based instruction scored higher than students without computers. The students also learned more in less time and liked their classes more when ICT-based instruction was included. (Sosin, Blecha, Agawal, Bartlett, Daniel, 2004) constructed a database of 67 sections of introductory economics, enrolling 3,986 students, taught by 30 instructors in 15 institutions in the United States of America during the spring and autumn semesters of 2002. They found positive impact on student performance due to ICT use.

6.5 ANALYSIS OF MEAN SCORES OF COURSE SATISFACTION

H5 There is no significant difference in the mean scores on course outcomes of prospective teachers exposed to different instructional treatments with respect to course satisfaction.

The analysis of mean scores was analysed using t- test. The obtained t-value on course satisfaction for Experimental and control groups has been given in table 6.9.

Table 6.13: t-ratio for difference in the post test mean score of experimental and control group on course satisfaction

Group	N	Mean	S.D	t-ratio	Remarks
Control	51	78.96	13.03		
Experimental	51	132.16	5.46	27.01**	Significant

** Significant at 0.01 level; * Significant at 0.05 level

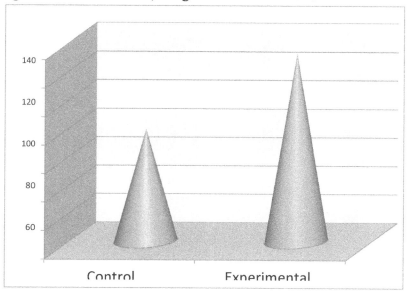

Figure 6.15: Bar diagram showing comparison of mean scores of experimental and control group on course satisfaction

Table 6.13 and fig. 6.15 reveals that experimental group achieved higher mean of 132.16 than that of control group which is 78.96 on course satisfaction after completing the course. The t- value for the difference is 27.01. This t-value is significant at 0.01 level of significance. Therefore, it may be interpreted that there exists a significant difference in the course outcomes of the two groups. Hence, the null hypothesis H5: There will be no significant difference in the mean gain scores on course satisfaction of the two groups, is rejected. The result indicates that the two groups were different on course satisfaction after the experimental treatment. It shows that Experimental group taught through ICT skills development program showed higher course satisfaction as compared to control group taught through conventional method.

6.5.1 DISCUSSION OF RESULTS OF COURSE OUTCOMES

H_5 was rejected as the t- ratio for the mean difference of scores of the two treatment group was found to significant at 0.01 level of confidence. With respect to course satisfaction that is one of component of course outcomes, t- ratio scores of the two treatment groups were found to be significant at 0.01 level. An examination of means indicates that Information and communication technology skills development program was superior to traditional method of teaching computer application. The present research suggested that students' course satisfaction influences their computer achievement in ICT skills development program. According to Bean and Bradley (1986), course satisfaction had a significant effect on the performance but the performance did not have a strong positive effect on course satisfaction. Results from this research supported their conclusion. Further, Astin (1993) suggested that satisfaction was an important intermediate outcome between students' level of motivation and their performance. Results from this research also supported his point of view that the course outcome was the mediator between students' levels of motivation and their performance. However Bean and Bradley (1986) also suggested that the relationship between course satisfaction and performance cannot be assumed as a one-way causal relationship. They believed that other factors also influence whether high level of satisfaction leads to strong performance or strong performance leads to high level of satisfaction. For example, the effects of performance on satisfaction may be different from students who emphasize on intellectual to those who emphasize on social life in campus. For students with intellectual emphasis, the higher grades usually lead to higher level of course satisfaction. On the other hand, for students with social life emphasis, higher course satisfaction usually leads to higher performance.

CHAPTER - VII
SUMMARY, FINDINGS AND EDUCATIONAL IMPLICATIONS

In the preceding chapters, introduction to variables of the study, review of related literature, emergence of the problem, objectives, hypotheses, delimitations, designs, tools used, data collections, procedure of the study, analysis of data and results were presented in detail. The present chapter contains summary, finding and implications of the study.

7.1 INTRODUCTION

The use of Technology in education is becoming an increasingly important part of higher and professional education (Wernet, Olliges, & Delicath, 2000; & Almekhlafi, 2006a, 2006b). Technology not only gives learners the opportunity to control their own pace of learning, but also provides them with ready access to a vast amount of information and knowledge over which the teacher has no control (Lam & Lawrence, 2002).Education is a light that shows the human beings the right direction to surge. The purpose of education is not just making a student literate but adds rationale thinking, knowledge ability and self sufficiency. When there is a willingness to change, there is hope for progress in any field.

Creativity can be developed and innovative ideas and benefits both students and teachers. The 21st century is dedicated to bring up a knowledge-based society in which required competencies strive to follow the extremely fast development of tools that are needed for Life Long Learning. But, the structure of teacher education is not suitable to handle the extent of changes progressing in our daily lives influencing the future generation of learners. Thus, there needs to be a sustainable flow of innovation continuously shaping government education in order to bring up a generation that can stand up to requirements within the future workforce. According to the Merriam Webster dictionary, innovation is merely "the introduction of something new" and Wikipedia adds very wisely, that "the central meaning of innovation relates to renewal or improvement, with novelty being a consequence of this improvement". Higher education plays a pivotal role in the development of a country, as it is viewed as a powerful means to build knowledge based society. In India, higher education imparted by universities is facing challenges in terms of Access, Equity and Quality.

Use of ICT for promoting education and development has always been a part of policy and plan documents on education.

Technology integration in the classroom has become an important aspect of successful teaching. It has triggered many researchers to investigate different aspects of such integration (Kotrlik & Redmann, 2005; Bauer and Kenton, 2005; Judson, 2006; Totter et al., 2006; ChanLin et al., 2006; Zhao, 2007; Gulbahar, 2007; Anderson and Maninger, 2007; Abbit and Klett, 2007; & Wood and Ashfield, 2008). This is because it allows students to learn more in less time and allows schools to focus on global learning environments if used appropriately. In addition, it could be an effective teaching tool when used to engage all students in the learning process (Almekhlafi, 2006). The wide spread technological advancement in the new knowledge economy has created increasingly more powerful ICTs and increasing demand on workers with advanced (ICT) skills. However, just because the technology is available does not mean everyone can get the training and develop skills in it. Those who cannot use necessary information and training, and cannot keep pace with technological revolution will be lag behind and vulnerable as knowledge economy has already wreaked havoc in unskilled and semi-skilled employment (Hull 2003). Research shows that there are increasing number of computers being used at home and an increasing number of technological devices available to schools (Goddard, 2002). Research documented teachers' use of computers for different purposes and objectives (Guha, 2000; Yildirim, 2000; & Rowand, 2000). Some teachers use computers for instructional purposes while others use them for both personal and instructional goals.

This rapid technological advancement has lead to the digital divide where it is generally understood as a multidimensional phenomenon encompassing three distinct aspects. The 'Global Divide' refers to the divergence of ICT access between developed and developing societies. The 'Social Divide' concerns the gap between the information rich and the poor in each nation. And lastly, within the online community, the 'democratic Divide' signifies the difference between those who do, and do not, use the panoply of digital resources and ICT to engage, mobilise and participate in social, cultural, educational, professional and economic aspects of life. The widening digital divide issue has aroused a concern all around the world. For the balanced and sustained development, countries and cities started to develop aforementioned initiatives and understand their responsibilities in respects of information resource sharing and narrowing the digital divide. The continuum of these initiatives and policies will likely be able to change the digital divide into a digital opportunity (Norris 2001).

Guha (2000) reported significant differences and positive correlations between teachers' present computer training, level of comfort, and computer usage in the classroom as compared to their previous training, comfort level, and usage. Bauer and Kenton (2005) found that teachers, who were highly educated and skilled with technology, were innovative and adept at overcoming obstacles, but they did not integrate technology on a consistent basis both as a teaching and learning tool. Results suggest that schools have not yet achieved true technology integration.

7.2 RATIONALE OF THE STUDY

Lim (2005) found that the use of ICT in teaching and learning allowed students to be active in finding information and build knowledge from information obtained by the chance to cross-link between knowledge of subjects without restricted by time and distance. Banerjee et al. (2004) present the results of a randomized policy evaluation carried out in two Indian States to improve the quality of education in urban slums. The authors found out that a computer assisted program, designed to reinforce mathematical skills, had a large and positive impact on math scores; however, the program did not produce positive spillovers to other subjects. Machin et al. (2006) evaluated whether changes in ICT investment had any causal impact on changes in educational outcomes in English schools over the period from 1999 to 2003. Moore (2005) summarised about the positive impact of ICT on pupils' learning such as increased students' motivation to stay on-task and drive them to behave better and produce high quality work. Besides, through ICT, students learnt more independently and did more works at a fast pace.

According to Kubiatko (2010), the results of students' attitudes toward ICT use in teaching and learning Science subject among high school students were based on statistical evaluation. Students seemed interested in using ICT in the Science subjects. Ong, Foo and Lee (2010) in their study revealed that the initiative of Malaysia Smart Schools promotes the use of ICT has created significant positive attitude towards Science among students. Anderson and Maninger (2007) investigated the changes in and factors related to students' technology-related abilities, beliefs, and intentions.

Statistically significant changes were found in students' perceived abilities, self-efficacy beliefs, value beliefs, and intentions to use software in their future classrooms. Students' self-efficacy, value beliefs, and intentions were moderately correlated with each other. Abilities were correlated with self-efficacy and computer access. The best predictors of intentions were self-efficacy beliefs, gender, and value beliefs Most of the previous research showed significant effect of ICT on the computer achievement of students.

Christensen and Knezek (2006) described computer self-efficacy as computer confidence in competence. Christensen (2002) revealed that teachers' competence with computer technology is a key factor of effective use of ICT in teaching. Peralta and Costa (2007) conducted a study on 20 teachers' competences and confidence regarding the use of ICT in classrooms. They revealed that in Italy, teachers' technical competence with technology is a factor of improving higher confidence in the use of ICT.

Research findings have found teachers incompetence with computer and technology integration among other factors has been responsible for the computer achievement. Improving computer self efficacy and technology integration beliefs and reversing the current negative trend in computer achievement through ICT skills development program is a major objective of this research.

7.3 STATEMENT OF THE PROBLEM

EFFECT OF INFORMATION AND COMMUNICATION TECHNOLOGY SKILLS DEVELOPMENT PROGRAM ON COMPUTER SELF EFFICACY, SELF REGULATION, TECHNOLOGY INTEGRATION BELIEFS AND COURSE OUTCOMES OF PROSPECTIVE TEACHERS

7.4 OBJECTIVES

The main objectives of the study were:

1. To develop and validate Information and Communication Technology (ICT) skills development program for prospective teachers.
2. To compare the effect of Information and Communication Technology (ICT) skills development program and traditional instruction on computer self efficacy of prospective teachers.

3. To compare the effect of Information and Communication Technology (ICT) skills development program and traditional instruction on self regulation of prospective teachers.
4. To compare the effect of Information and Communication Technology (ICT) skills development program and traditional instruction on technology integration beliefs of prospective teachers.
5. To compare the effect of Information and Communication Technology (ICT) skills development program and traditional instruction on course outcomes with respect to Computer achievement, performance and satisfaction of prospective teachers.

7.5 HYPOTHESES

H_1 There is no significant difference in the mean gain scores on computer self efficacy of prospective teachers exposed to different instructional treatments.

Further hypothesis were formulated to analyse mean gain scores on computer self efficacy with respect to the three domains.

The two instructional treatments yield equal mean difference scores on: $H_{1.01}$ Beginning skills

$H_{1.02}$ File and Software skills

$H_{1.03}$ Advancing Skills

H_2 There is no significant difference in the mean gain scores on self regulation of prospective teachers exposed to different instructional treatments.

Further hypothesis were formulated to analyse mean gain scores on self regulation with respect to the seven domains.

The two instructional treatments yield equal mean difference scores on: $H_{2.01}$ Receiving

$H_{2.02}$ Evaluating $H_{2.03}$ Triggering

$H_{2.04}$ Searching

$H_{2.05}$ Formulating

$H_{2.06}$ Implementing

$H_{2.07}$ Assessing

H_3 There is no significant difference in the mean gain scores on technology integration beliefs of prospective teachers exposed to different instructional treatments.

H_4 There is no significant difference in the mean gain scores on course outcome of prospective teachers exposed to different instructional treatments with respect to computer achievement.

H_5 There is no significant difference in the mean scores on course outcome of prospective teachers exposed to different instructional treatments with respect to course satisfaction.

7.6 DELIMITATION OF THE STUDY

1) The present study was conducted on B.Ed students of Indo Global College of Education, Abhipur, Distt. Mohali and International Divine College of Education, Ratwara Sahib, Mullanpur which are affiliated to Punjabi University, Patiala.

2) The study was limited to only ICT components of B.Ed curriculum of Punjabi University, Patiala.

3) The Instructional treatment was limited to thirty five sessions of forty minutes duration each.

4) The course outcomes were limited to two aspects computer achievement and satisfaction with instructional program.

7.7 SAMPLE

For the current investigation, the population was the prospective teachers of education colleges of Punjab. A sample of prospective teachers was purposively selected. The procedure of selecting the sample given below:

Prospective teachers of education colleges and sample distribution

The sample was selected at two levels for education colleges and prospective teachers viz.

(i) Bachelor of Education (B.Ed) college sample
(ii) Prospective teachers sample

    (i) Bachelor of Education (B.Ed) college sample

Based on the criteria of permission from college principal regarding conducting experimental study, two education colleges were chosen for the study viz.

(ii) Prospective teachers sample

From the selected private education colleges, 102 prospective teachers were randomly chosen from two private education colleges. The colleges were compared with regards to the criteria that college has almost same classroom climate, physical facilities, teacher taught ratio, sex ratio, digital lab etc.

Table 5.1: College wise distribution of sample

S. NO.	NAME OF COLLEGE
1.	Indo Global College of Education, Abhipur, Distt. Mohali
2.	International Divine College of Education, Ratwara sahib, Mullanpur

DIAGRAMMATIC PRESENTATION OF THE STUDY

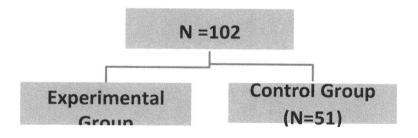

7.8 TOOLS USED

The following tools were used for collecting data:

Tools are the techniques which are appropriate for the collection of certain types of evidence or information for conducting the research. The tools used for the present study are given below:

1. Information and Communication Technology (ICT) skills development program (Developed and Validated by investigator)
2. Computer Self Efficacy Scale (Cassidy & Eachus, 2002)

3. Self Regulation Scale (Brown, Miller, & Lawendowski, 1999)
4. Technology integration beliefs scale (Developed &Validated by investigator)
5. Course outcomes test viz.
    5.1 Computer achievement (Developed and validated by investigator)
    5.2 Course Satisfaction Questionnaire (Frey, Yankelov and Faul, 2003).

7.9 STATISTICAL TECHNIQUES USED

The following statistical techniques have been employed to analyze the data obtained from the experiment in order to test the hypotheses.

(i) Descriptive statistics techniques viz. Mean, standard deviation, skewness and kurtosis were used to determine the nature of distribution of the scores.

(ii) Graphical presentations were used for visual perception of the data.

(iii) t-ratios were calculated for testing the significance of difference between the mean scores of different groups on variables under study.

7.10 RESULTS

The data was analysed using descriptive and inferential statistics. In order to test the significance of difference between means t- ratio were computed. The raw data was statistically treated and processed on Statistical Package for Social Sciences (SPSS) 20. The result and interpretation are given in Chapter-VI.

7.11 MAJOR FINDINGS

The data obtained from the experiment were statistically analyzed and the following results were obtained which are described under following sub-headings:

Findings Pertaining to Computer Self Efficacy

The experimental group students yielded better mean gains through information and communication technology skills development program than control group students taught through traditional method on computer self efficacy and following dimensions:

$H_{1.01}$ Beginning skills

$H_{1.02}$ File and Software skills

$H_{1.03}$ Advancing Skills

Finding Pertaining to Self Regulation

The students of experimental group yielded better mean gains through information and communication technology skills development program than control group students taught through traditional method on self regulation and its dimensions:

$H_{2.01}$ Receiving $H_{2.02}$

  Evaluating $H_{2.03}$

Triggering $H_{2.04}$

Searching $H_{2.05}$

Formulating $H_{2.06}$

Implementing $H_{2.07}$

Assessing

Findings Pertaining to Technology Integration Beliefs

The students of experimental group yielded better mean gains through information and communication technology skills development program than control group students taught through traditional method on technology integration beliefs.

Findings Pertaining to Computer Achievement Test

The experimental group students yielded better mean gains through information and communication technology skills development program than control group students taught through traditional method on computer achievement test.

Findings Pertaining to Course Satisfaction Questionnaire

The experimental group students yielded better mean gains through information and communication technology skills development program than control group students taught through traditional method on course satisfaction.

7.12 EDUCATIONAL IMPLICATIONS

The findings of present study have some very important implication for improving the quality of instruction in acquisition of ICT skills. The day may not be far when most Indian students will have access to both educational technology and instructional technology. The results of this study suggest that administrators should place emphasis on building student and teachers' perception of their ability to use technology with a view to transform classroom practices. In order to encourage teachers to integrate technology into teaching and learning, they ought to be given opportunities to acquire basic technology skills such as the use of presentation and word processing tools and at the same time, organize courses on the strategies to infuse technology for pedagogical purposes.

❖ Students need to be prompted to make use of internet for updating their knowledge and general awareness skills.

❖ Social science teachers need to be made aware about the benefits of ICT usage.

❖ Training courses for computer applications should be organized in the schools.

❖ Both pre service and in-service teachers should be properly trained to integrate technology in their daily classroom processes.

❖ In service computer courses to enhance confidence in computer usage need to be organized.

❖ School Principals should motivate the senior teachers to adapt technology in teaching.

❖ Competitions focusing on teaching social studies topic through the computers need to be organized.

❖ Administrators should provide internet enabled laptops to students from humble backgrounds for free or, at substantial rates, so that they are also able to keep up with the world of ever growing knowledge, example Akash.

❖ Teachers need to facilitate and adjust their instructional strategies that will optimize their students' learning, they need to be provided with the relevant skills and possess successful experiences in technology use at the teacher training stage.

❖ In order to build up computer self-efficacy, teachers need to compulsorily integrate technology to teaching.

Finally, because perceptions do not remain static, student teachers who perceive themselves as adept users of technology may soon experience limitations if they do not keep abreast with advances in the technologies relevant to them. Teachers and students must not only be able to use the technology present today but be prepared to handle the innovations in the technology world in future.

7.13 SUGGESTIONS FOR FURTHER STUDY

(i) The present study may be extended at degree college and university level in different subjects to find out the effectiveness of information and communication technology skills development program.

(ii) The present study may be conducted with other variables viz. Interest, motivation, retention, social skills study habits, techno-stress and locus of control to different age groups.

(iii) Researches can be conducted on a wider sample for more valid generalizations. Also the researches can be conducted for subjects other than computer, to have a comprehensive picture.

(iv) Comparative studies of ICT skills development program may be conducted with other methods of instructions at different grade level.

(v) The same study can be conducted for longer duration to examine the effects on non cognitive variable like social skills or some personality variable which take more time to bring about the change.

(vi) Studies intended to measure the effectiveness of strategies in terms of competence of teachers and student teachers to implement the models in classroom situations also may also be undertaken.

Copyright

Copyright © 2020by C.miya

All rights reserved.

No part of this publication may be reproduced, distributed, or transmitted in any form or by any means, including photocopying, recording, or other electronic or mechanical methods, without the prior written permission of the publisher. For permission requests, contactc. miya.in@gmail.comFor privacy reasons, some names, locations, and dates may have been changed.

Book Cover by S.Jaffer

Illustrations by A.Rohith

S

Publisher Notes:

This edition was inspired by other works, and a portion of its content was derived from public domain sources. Using manuscripts, select texts, and illustrative images from public domain archives, C.Miya created, edited, and published the EBook edition. Members can obtain this eBook from our website for personal use. No commercial storage, transmission, or reverse engineering of this file is permitted.

Acknowledgments

I would like to express my gratitude to everyone who has helped me with this endeavour. During the course of the project, I am grateful to them for providing me with aspirational guidance, invaluably constructive criticism, and friendly advise. I owe them an enormous debt of gratitude for the fact that they were honest and provided insightful commentary on a variety of topics pertaining to the project. At InfoTech, Mr. Jaffer and Mrs. Sameena have been quite helpful, and I am grateful to them both for it. In addition, I would like to express my gratitude to Mr. Ahmed, who served as my project's external adviser and works for the Ahmed company; Ms. Sultana; and everyone else who assisted me in obtaining the necessary resources and an environment that was suitable to the completion of my project. I would also like to credit the person who inspired me to write this book. Thank you, C.Miya

CPSIA information can be obtained
at www.ICGtesting.com
Printed in the USA
BVHW041431310523
665082BV00001B/42